English Stories for Verbally Talented Students

English Stories
for Verbally Talented Students

ⓒ 이숙희, 2019
1판 1쇄 인쇄__2019년 12월 20일
1판 1쇄 발행__2019년 12월 30일

편저자__이숙희
펴낸이__홍정표
펴낸곳__글로벌콘텐츠
　　　　등록__제25100-2008-000024호
　　　　이메일__edit@gcbook.co.kr

공급처__(주)글로벌콘텐츠출판그룹
　　　　대표__홍정표 이사__김미미 편집__김봄 이예진 권군오 홍명지 기획·마케팅__노경민 이종훈
　　　　주소__서울특별시 강동구 풍성로 87-6(성내동) 전화__02) 488-3280 팩스__02) 488-3281
　　　　홈페이지__http://www.gcbook.co.kr

값 13,500원
ISBN 979-11-5852-267-4 13740

English Stories for Verbally Talented Students

이숙희 편저

글로벌콘텐츠

Content

머리말

오늘 날 영어 교실에는 다양한 특성, 관심, 잠재 능력을 가진 학생들이 섞여 있으며 언어 우수아도 그 중 일부이다. 언어 우수아에게 있어서 언어는 의사소통이라는 기능적 측면 보다는 추론, 분석, 해석, 비판 등의 고등 사고력 측면에서 흥미를 끈다. 때문에 언어 우수아들은 외국어에서도 언어 자체 보다는 의미가 강조되는 수업을 선호한다.

문학은 여러 자료 중에서도 언어 우수아의 고등 사고 능력을 가장 쉽게 촉진할 수 있는 자료이다. 문학은 상징, 복선, 역설, 아이러니 등 사고의 복잡한 장치들을 두루 담고 있기 때문이다. 만약 그 장치 및 내용들이 언어 우수아의 흥미를 끌 수 있다면 그들은 다른 장르의 글들에서 보다도 훨씬 더 적극적으로 외국어의 장벽을 뛰어넘고자 시도할 것이다. 이런 방식으로 그들은 자연스럽게 외국어 수준도 높여나간다.

이 책은 향후 자신의 교실에서 언어 우수아를 지도해야 할 예비교사들, 즉 사범대 영어교육과 학생들을 위한 책이다. 예비교사들은 읽기 자료 선정에서부터 학습 과정과 결과물 산출에 이르기까지 언어 우수아의 고등 사고력을 자극하고 강화해 줄 질적 심화 프로그램을 지속적으로 창안해야 한다. 이 책은 문학 텍스트를 중점적으로 다룸으로써 예비교사로 하여금 언어 우수자의 교육에 대비하도록 하였다.

이 책은 필자가 쓴 논문 'Teaching English for Verbally Talented Students'로 시작한다. 이 논문은 언어 우수자의 특성을 세부적으로 밝히고 그들을 위한 의미 중심적 영어교육이 필요한 이유를 논한 글로서 이 책의 이론적 바탕이 된다. 이어서 총 12편의 영어 단편 소설이 수록되어 있다. 이런 작품들을 통하여 예비교사들은 문학이 가진 유추, 분석, 해석, 판단 등 고등사고력을 배양하고 그런 사고력을 촉발하는 문학적 장치를 보다 정확하게 가려냄으로써 향후 언어우수아들을 지도할 수 있는 역량을 갖추게 될 것이다. 예비교사들이 다양한 교실에서 보다 창의적이고 흥미로운 방법으로 문학을 활용한 영어교육을 실천하는 데 이 책이 작은 기여를 할 수 있기 바란다.

English Stories for **Verbally** Talented **Students**

Teaching English
for Verbally Talented Students

I. Introduction

The Korean Education Ministry announced that from 2008 it will provide special education for the 5% high ability students in public schools. Considering that most developed countries have already started investing social concern and effort in fostering young brilliant talents as a globally competitive national resource, such a decision of the Korean government seems proper for its future. As is already known publicly, gifted education has become a competitive field among countries. The launch of Sputnik in 1957 sparked the impetus for such competition. Shocked by Russia's unexpected lead in scientific technology, the American government recognized its relevant neglect in developing young excellence and began to put great efforts in it, which resulted in remarkable theoretical and practical achievements. After vigorous research of how to identify the talented and how underrepresented and unserved they are in regular education programs, American gifted education field has reached to the stage of creating appropriate curricula for them.

For the last decade, gifted education has been also carried out in Korea and attained some remarkable achievement in the science areas. Meanwhile, verbal arts talents were neither properly identified nor provided with a well-designed curriculum. Such relevant neglect in verbal arts talents compared to the sciences is not only limited to Korea but a general phenomenon. It is because verbal talent is more elusive to identify and hard to prove its social value. However, as Gardner (1983) delineated, verbal talent exists as a distinct separate intellectual domain of the 7 Multiple Intellects. It is also of a valuable social resource, especially in a postfordic and a heavily intellect-based society that requires creative thinking to an unpreceded extent.

Another suspicion of educational possibility for the verbal talent is that it is difficult to be nurtured by education. Recent research, however, shows that even though gains are not as dramatic as in mathematics or sciences, educational intervention in language arts has brought about significant growth of students' ability in inference, reading comprehension, vocabulary, and writing skills (Lynch & Mills, 1990, pp.375-6). In spite of this strong possibility of developing verbal talent, current curricula and teaching models in prestigious Korean secondary schools for verbal talents seem not to show any meaningful change for them.

To be truly responsive to talented students' needs and characteristics, the curriculum for them should go beyond 'acceleration' or 'compact' to 'enrichment,' which means a qualitative differentiation rather than quantitative rearrangement of the given subject content. The purpose of this study is to locate English learning properly in the whole curriculum of talented students. To do this, it will emphasize English as a language rather than as a foreign language. Like it or not, English is one of the most important languages used globally. Talented students, scientifically or verbally, need to learn English as a communicative tool to receive or generate knowledge. Traditionally, English has been taught in Korean secondary schools separated from other disciplines, even other humanities. Without any interdisciplinary linkage to other subjects, English class has focused on building linguistic skills for communicative fluency. The aspect of humanities of English learning tended to be simply ignored before its emphasis on linguistic skills. Thus, even while enhancing creativity has emerged as a strong visible issue in general Korean schooling with more emphasis in the gifted education area, it does not extend to English courses. Such a decisive isolation of English class from other disciplines, especially from other humanities, and lack of creative activities in the course have high possibility of demotivating particular students with distinct talents in verbal arts, because too self-evident or basal learning usually causes them to lose their learning enthusiasm. This paper aims to clarify the necessity that in terms of high ability students education English teaching should be ultimately integrated in the broader realm of verbal arts even in secondary education and to suggest some presumptions to make it successful.

II. Educational Implications of Verbal Talent

According to a holistic view of education, education can be successful only when the three major components of the learner, the teacher, and the curriculum dynamically interact. Thus, the practical understanding of the learner is the first factor to be considered in talented education if it aims at true differentiation, which means that correct identification and diagnosis of talent should go first before designing enrichment. Then, what students can be recognized as verbally talented? Learners who have scored high on tests of verbal intelligence? Or those who show unusual ability of linguistic skills such as creative writing? These assumptions show that verbal talent is hard to be clearly defined. Michael, an earlier scholar in this field, observed: "Gifted persons may be supposed, therefore, to need superior skill in the use of language and superior understanding of, and familiarity with, the media of language expression" (Michael, 1958, p.280). Michael discussed the language areas as including the expressive arts of writing and speaking, semantic understanding, the structure of language, and reading, listening, and watching the screen. More recently, Gardner(1983) identified verbal talent as a person who skillfully uses language as a tool and Jane Piitro added "children who do produce work in writing on the adult level of competence" (Piitro, 1992, p.387).

According to these scholars, verbal talent is associated with specific linguistic ability, that is, outstanding potential in some verbal area such as creative writing, poetry, dramatic arts, and so on. In the meantime, more recent scholars in the gifted education field tend to associate verbal talent with verbal reasoning rather than specific linguistic skill. They argue that high ability learners in language arts are distinguished not only in language skills but also in high order thinking. In fact, most curricular builders for verbal talents these days adopt this perspective of verbal talent, with which this study agrees.

Another important thing in regards with understanding high

ability learners is their attitudes toward the subject. Talent is not the concept limited to ability; it rather goes to interest, intensity, learning style, and creativity. High ability learners are different not only in their intellectual ability but also in their extraordinary intensity and creativity toward the task. Renzulli (2004) says:

Our field does not glorify the copyists of the high level replicators of knowledge and art, and only rarely does history remember people who have made accidental discoveries. Rather, our focus has been on men and women who have purposefully made it their business to attack the unsolved problems of mankind. It is for this reason that educators of the gifted constantly invoke such names as Einstein, Edison, Curie, Beethoven, Duncan, and a host of others who have made creative contributions to their chosen fields of endeavor. If mankind's creative producers and solvers of real problems are constantly held up before us as idealized prototypes of the "gifted person." then it seems nothing short of common sense to use their modus operandi to construct a model for educating our most promising young people.(49)

For Renzulli the most important characteristic of the gifted is their intense attachment to "the unsolved problems of mankind." Thus, his famous enrichment program for the gifted, Triad, mainly focuses on the process to stimulate students' creativity through which the gifted students can generate new knowledge to solve "the unsolved problems". Renzulli's effort is remarkable in that it aims at the real creativity and thus brings out qualitative differentiation in incorporating curricula for the gifted by embracing the enrichment of process in it. However, as the quote shows, Renzulli's cases are generally biased towards science or art with language arts somewhat neglected. It is because verbally talented students mobilize different intellect and modes of thinking from scientifically talented ones; whereas science emphasizes curiosity, objectivity, and problem-solving in the process, language arts requires high order thinking, reasoning and construction of meaning. For this reason, more specific characteristics of verbal talent should be considered for verbal talent curriculum, of which the following three are consented to be most important.

The first prominent characteristic of the general verbal talent is precocity (VanTassel-Baska, 1996, p.14). For talented learners, language development typically occurs early and appears to be spontaneous. After their natural and spontaneous mastery of basic reading skills, they tend to move fast toward more advanced levels of reading and thinking. Thus the curriculum for them needs to be highly advanced both in the quantity and quality of reading materials.

The intensity of the gifted learners is the second characteristic of curricular interest (VanTassel-Baska, 1996, p.15). If they find their task intriguing, the talented often concentrate on it for a long time until they attain a certain level of accomplishment that may satisfy themselves. As numerous studies (e.g., Krapp, 1989; Renninger, 1989) have already demonstrated, individual interests have profound influences on learning and it is more true for the talented. Thus the curriculum for this group should include highly fascinating tasks to stimulate their strong intensity.

Complexity is the third characteristic to consider in curriculum development (VanTassel-Baska, 1996, p.15). Gifted learners love to challenge hard work to activate their multiple capabilities in a simultaneous way. Even at young ages, they love to solve the problem that requires high-level thinking in their own way, which means they love to learn for themselves. This is why too much instruction could be "insulting" for the talented. (VanTassel-Baska, 2004, p.53)

III. Curriculum Models for Verbal Talent

As the characteristics of gifted and talented were clarified as above, gifted education specialists have enthusiastically tried to create an appropriate curriculum for them. Thus, over the past

30 years, curriculum studies has been a major issue in the field with the proliferation of books and articles on the subject, which can be categorized into three models: the content model, the process-product model, and the epistemological model (VanTassel-Baska, 2004, pp.3-10).

The content model emphasizes the rapid mastery of content in a given domain. In this model, students are pre-tested and then given appropriate materials that are organized by the intellectual hierarchy of content. This is why the content model is also called as a diagnostic-prescriptive instructional model. The content-based programs are highly effective when educational settings such as competent classroom manager to implement the individualized program properly are satisfied. The approach, however, has not been particularly valued by many educators of the gifted because of its heavy dependence on able teachers. The more serious problem of the content model lies in its failure of properly integrating the potential and learning styles of the talented into education. It just requires the same learning skills and strategies of the talented as it does of all learners in the school context. Despite these problems, however, it is true that the content model has been utilized effectively by the talent search programs (e.g., Keating, 1976; Benbow and Stanley, 1993).

The process-product model, popularized by Renzulli through

the Enrichment Triad in 1977, offered program pioneers in the field a model for nurturing talent regardless of the specific area of ability. This model places heavy emphasis on students' learning process and creative products including higher-order thinking skills, problem-finding, problem-solving and relevant real-world products. Seeking to engage the student in exploring, investigating, and producing knowledge, this model put the student in contact with adult experts in a given domain. Renzulli's model has been accepted as a true differentiated curriculum model that allows the gifted children to develop their creativity to its full degree, especially in the domain of cognitive science, through calling for higher-order thinking skills, relevant real-world products, and an emphasis on different modes of thinking.

The concept model, epistemological model, is the one most recently developed whose underlying tenet is concern for the nature and structure of knowledge itself. With emphases on understanding and application of systems of knowledge rather than the individual segments of the given discipline, this model encourages students to get the general concept of knowledge which can be continuously amplified by the new learning experiences. Many writers in the field of gifted education have advocated the epistemological approach to curriculum for the gifted (e.g., Ward, 1961; Hayes-Jacob, 1981; Maker, 1982;

Tannenbaum, 1993), because this model is very effective with gifted learners for several reasons. First of all, with its whole emphasis on interdisciplinary interactions, it can effectively respond to the gifted student who has unusually keen powers to see and understand interrelationships among disciplines. Second, concept curriculum can provide the gifted with epistemological schemata that they can apply to structuralize any new segments of knowledge. Such capability of metacognition can also make good influences on their confidence and ownership in learning. The third merit of the concept model is that it provides a basis for students' understanding the creative as well as the intellectual process. Since the model requires the students to delve into in-depth structure of knowledge rather than self-evident facts, they are consistently put into the condition of active learning. Through this process, the students naturally practice to find creative ways to the problems and develop their creativity.

IV. Integrated Curriculum Model

In order to implement an appropriate curriculum, there must be concern for the faithful translation of sound models for curriculum and instruction into an action research arena where effectiveness can be continually tested. The above three curriculum models have been tested and proven effective in various domains. What was most advocated and widely translated in American schooling is Renzulli's model, the process-product model. With deep consideration of student interest, learning intensity, and creativity, he presented a radically differentiated curriculum for the gifted. In spite of this achievement, this model does show some problems. Critics contend that the process-product models tend to devalue core content elements in the traditional curriculum and to overvalue the independent learning strategies of the student. They also point that the process-product models reveal significant problems when applied to disciplines where knowledge itself is a rich substance as the basis of generating new ideas or issues. Language arts is one of them. It is the Integrated Curriculm Model(ICM) that has been introduced as an alternative model to solve such serious lack on the part of Renzulli's Triad. First proposed by VanTassel-Baska in 1986 and further explicated in the subsequent publication (VanTassel-Baska, 1993), this model synthesizes the three approaches mentioned above to curriculum development: content, process, and concept. On the basis of diagnostic-prescriptive approaches employed to ensure new learning as opposed to remedial instruction, ICM emphasizes advanced content knowledge that frames

curriculum. Much research has already demonstrated that the relevance between high-ability in L1 and L2 is significantly high. For example, English is the subject-matter secondly favored by talented students of Korean language (박수자, 2004, p.37). All these findings prove that the verbally talented students in L1 are likely to be interested in L2 and use the same learning strategies in second language acquisition as they utilize in L1. Gardner's multiple intelligence theory can be a good explanation for the reason why a brilliant student in L1 has high chance of being good at L2 as well. According to Gardner (1983), there exists not only a general intelligence but multiple intelligences(MI) found in different parts of the brain: logical-mathematical, linguistic, spatial, bodily-kinesthetic, musical, interpersonal, and intrapersonal intelligences. These seven intelligences are innate and independent and everyone has potential in each of these areas. Gardner's MI theory proves that it is the same intelligence, linguistic intelligence that works in learning both of L1 and L2.

As CLT became a central trend of English education, literature has been drastically expelled from the class because of its use of language in a more complex and abstract way. Literary language was understood not in harmony with common daily language that CLT aims at. It is only in the last decade that a remarkable upsurge of interest in using literature in the EFL classroom has started. Recent developments in the field of critical theory such as structuralism and reader-response theory contributed on such revival of literature by providing some important insights for teachers to introduce more enriched literary materials and programs into the language classroom. Some new educational theories also supported the trend. For example, a holistic view in education that emphasizes learning as an interactive process of the learner, task, and the context (Novak & Gowin, 1984) made sense that to succeed, education should provide not a standardized curriculum but different repertories with positive respect for the student. Constructivism also emphasizes the process of learning as a series of communicative processes between learners and texts. For constructivists, learning is an act of construction ___ an act in which learners build meanings through bringing their relevant knowledge to the task (e.g., Ackerman, 1991; Bransford, Barclay, & Franks, 1972; Frederiksen, 1975; Spiro, 1977, 1980; Spivey, 1987, 1990). This view also indicates the need for a student-centered learning program in which the learner's prior knowledge and ownership are highly regarded.

Owing to various social factors such as English learning for university entrance examination, English teaching in Korea has been designed and practiced in a single national standard model. In this model, students' individual interests, abilities, attitudes, and learning styles have been rarely considered. To attain the national goal in English education, EFL has generally focused on objective and cognitive sides of language teaching. Repeated practices of simple sentences for daily communications, controlled learning goals and processes, and plain repertories are the matter-of-fact results of this model. As mentioned before, these teaching methods are not in harmony with verbally talented learners' learning characteristics who tend to quickly lose their early curiosity with repeated busywork, which lacks any depth or complexity even if it is a subject of their interest.

Now it is the time to develop a proper EFL program which can respond to the needs of some special students and maximize their potential through learning. This new program should regard learners' affective traits as well as cognitive ones, which can properly stimulate their learning motivation of foreign language. As for the verbally talented students, literature can be a strong possibility. Since literary competence is their common potential, they have already had good schemata for reading literature. As Gardner's MI theory proves, literary and linguistic intelligence, working on the level of general language semiotics, goes ahead of the difference of any specific foreign language. Talented students with high literary and linguistic ability easily adapt their general verbal schemata to foreign language literature and enjoy it. Literature also leads them to various vocabularies and expressions, which enables automatic learning regarded as the most natural and effective method of language acquisition. Last, literature also contributes to develop the creative communication skills of the students. Verbal talents are excellent in working intertextually to generate their own meaning. Interacting with literary texts, they become actively engaged with creating meaning rather than passively consuming them. This is how verbal talents become more creative constructors as well as creative communicators through language learning. This paper does not argue that such learning process needs to be introduced into all EFL classrooms; rather, it argues for the need of some new EFL programs tailored for students with high literary competence and aptitude. Considering all this, we can conclude that the following are the pivotal elements to be embodied when incorporating a new EFL program for the verbal talent.

First, reading materials should be rich and rigorous. In the wake of communicative language teaching, literature was continuously regarded as inauthentic. Thus, basal reading texts with no ambiguity of meaning took the place of literature in reading area. Even when literary texts were ever introduced as reading materials, they were so simplified and made level-appropriate to avoid misunderstanding and abstractness. All these basal and self-evident reading materials can hardly motivate the verbally talented, because they are only interested in challenging materials with complexity and depth.

Traditionally in the study of second language comprehension, the emphasis has been almost exclusively on the language to be comprehended and not on the comprehender. In this view, readability was decided on the level of linguistic skills. However, reading involves more than the simple decoding of linguistic form. It is rather an active process wherein the reader brings his or her prior knowledge to the text. Verbally talented students have abundant prior knowledge related with various topics which makes their general reading comprehension much easier. They even have a set of very sophisticated schemata that efficiently organize, select, and connect meanings. Thus, when selecting reading materials for the verbal talent, readability needs to be decided not just on the level of linguistic ability but on the level of cognitive ability.

Second, high-order thinking should be emphasized. Those with verbal talent generally operate at a much higher level of thinking than his/her age peers. Therefore, EFL for verbal talents needs to include the domain of verbal reasoning such as inference, analysis, application, and critical evaluation.

Although it has been neglected all the while in EFL, reasoning is a very important factor for verbally talented students not only to develop their potentiality but also their English language competence. Since reasoning is their typical learning style as well as ability, they can learn English in an easier and more interesting way through reasoning. Reasoning is also important for them to build real in-depth communicative competence. Advanced-level communication is a complex and abstract activity itself where one should call for all clues from one's knowledge to share informations or negotiate in the smartest way.

Even foreign language learning should not exclude the desire and aptitude of verbal talent for such advanced communication. Traditional EFL classes usually did not require students for complex process of meaning negotiation, paying regard to their English language deficit. This resulted in tedious and boring communications which allow no creative meaning construction. As mentioned previously, it is mechanical or too obvious learning that the talented students are least interested in. Even EFL needs to consider the strong ownership of the learners in communicative activities with which they can play a role of an active creator of meaning rather than a passive receiver. In this sense, various reasoning models such as Paul's need to be positively incorporated into the EFL programs for the talented students.

Third, inquiry-based learning process should be emphasized. Bruner(1986) stated that education needs to bring learners to a growing edge of competence. The very nature of the questions can provide just the help for the student to extend his or her edge of potential. Through the presentation of the hypothetical nature of knowledge, its uncertainty, its invitation to further thought, education can provoke the student's potentiality of verbal reasoning to extend to its possible maximum. This is why even in EFL classroom, verbal talent needs to be asked fat questions related with critical and creative thinking, not just being limited to skinny questions about the correct meaning of texts.

The questions provided in traditional EFL classes are usually "skinny questions." These questions are provided to check whether students have comprehended the correct meaning of the text. If their answers to these questions deviate from the obviously controled answers, they are likely to be said wrong. However, verbally talented learners are more interested in open ended texts through which they can generate their own meaning. Considering that meaning does not come from incoming data of the text but from their high-order cognitive schemata, EFL needs to employ different types of questions from the language-driven skinny questions. "Fat questions" can be a solution for this. "Fat questions', including questions about the purpose of the text, its implications for the real world, and its relevance to one's life, are good opportunities for the young student to try out extended modes of inquiry to generate their own meaning. These fat questions may be practiced in the form of writing or discussion.

Fourth, interdisciplinary perspective should be included. For the verbally talented students, English is just a tool on the basis of which they may explore other humanities, since most of them will be employed in creative, critical, or scholarly works in the future rather than in translation or interpretation fields. Thus, their main goal is set to attaining a certain epistemological system of the knowledge relevant to their concern and creating their own new knowledge. For successful education, EFL should take such ultimate learning goals of students into prior consideration and incorporate them in its curriculum. In reality, too strong an emphasis on English acquisition has often brought out misunderstandings in the true object of learning a foreign language; language itself has become an end of learning rather than a communicative tool. Moreover, English education is isolated and compartmentalized, to use Spiro's (1980) term, being not related to other texts. The best answer to this problem is to introduce an interdisciplinary perspective in EFL. To do this, reading materials first of all should be selected according to the criteria of closeness to students' real problems. Reading explanations or issues of their concern in English may contribute to a double goal: building knowledge in a specific domain as well as learning English. The strong interdisciplinary bond of EFL to their main domain of interest may also respond to students' affective needs by ensuring what they do in the English classroom is relevant and meaningful to their own lives.

VI. Conclusion

By its nature, foreign language teaching tends to be approached only from its objective and cognitive sides, which is even true in Korea. For a long time, English education in Korea has emphasized on English language skills. Daily expressions and factual reading materials which can function on the clear dimension of linguistics and thus can avoid metaphysical confusion or ambiguity are more favored in English class. In such prescribed and controlled classroom conditions, students are expected to practice simple common expressions repeatedly. It is no doubt that such teaching methods can work very effectively in foreign language classes for certain students. The real problem happens, however, when they are uniformly adopted for all students including verbally talented students.

In order to provide students with appropriate curricula that can respond to their cognitive and affective needs, EFL, like other disciplines, has to consider their aptitudes, interests, and attitudes as the most important educational factors. Without such efforts, formal education in the nationally prescribed lockstep can be often not only invalid but also a torturous procedure for some students. Verbally talented students are motivated only when they are allowed to participate in creative communication with the text. With good literary schemata that they have already developed, they can interact with text and construct their own meaning. In this respect, literature is an excellent reading material for them. Literature has been doubted for its appropriateness in EFL, for it uses language in a unique way rather than commonly and prefers multi-layered or contradictory meanings to plain messages. For this reason, in EFL more obvious and factual reading materials have replaced literary texts. However, the abstractness and complexity of literature itself can motivate verbal talents rather than demotivate them, because it means the high possibility for them to explore and construct meanings.

In spite of its primary emphasis on communicative ability, CLT seems to remain on the semi-communicative stage. This is because the communications presented by CLT are often simulated situations with the real social context of language being removed. Students, especially the ones with high-order thinking ability, are not likely to participate in such articulated conversations with willingness or ownership. Instead, they easily feel bored with the flat activities that never suggest any kind of dramatic experience of engaging, exploring, and changing oneself through communication. To counter this situation, EFL should introduce new curricula and teaching methods. This does not mean that all traditional ways are wrong; it just means that we should develop some different English programs for students with special verbal ability in order to truly serve them, not only as independent individuals but also as valuable social resources.

A Rice Sandwich

Sandra Cisneros

Sandra Cisneros (1954–) is an American writer best known for her acclaimed first novel *The House on Mango Street* (1984) and her subsequent short story collection *Woman Hollering Creek and Other Stories* (1991). She grew up in a context of cultural hybridity and economic inequality that endowed her with unique stories to tell. Cisneros's early life provided many experiences she would later draw on as a writer: she grew up as the only daughter in a family of six brothers, which often made her feel isolated, and the constant migration of her family between Mexico and the USA instilled in her the sense of "always straddling two countries . . . but not belonging to either culture." Cisneros's work deals with the formation of Chicana identity, exploring the challenges of being caught between Mexican and Anglo-American cultures, facing the misogynist attitudes present in both these cultures, and experiencing poverty. For her insightful social critique and powerful prose style, Cisneros has achieved recognition far beyond Chicano and Latino communities, to the extent that *The House on Mango Street* has been translated worldwide and is taught in American classrooms as a coming-of-age novel. Cisneros has held a variety of professional positions, working as a teacher, a counselor, a college recruiter, a poet-in-the-schools, and an arts administrator, and has maintained a strong commitment to community and literary causes. In 1998 she established the Macondo Foundation, which provides socially conscious workshops for writers, and in 2000 she founded the Alfredo Cisneros Del Moral Foundation, which awards talented writers connected to Texas. Cisneros currently resides in San Antonio, Texas.

The House on Mango Street is written from the perspective of teenage Latina, Esperanza Cordero, who struggles with her life in a Chicano and Puerto Rican neighborhood of Chicago. Esperanza wishes to escape her impoverished life in her small red house on Mango Street to then return one day to rescue her loved ones as well. The novel combines old Mexican traditions with modern American customs and explores the plight of marginalized Latinos struggling to survive in a dominantly white country. The book has earned many awards and accolades, and is considered to be a modern classic of Chicana literature. The story begins with Esperanza, the protagonist, describing how her family arrived at the house on Mango Street. Before the family settled in their new house, they moved around frequently. The reader develops a sense of Esperanza's observant and descriptive nature as she begins the novel with descriptions of minute behaviors and observations about her family members. The novel also includes the stories of many of Esperanza's neighbors, providing a picture of the neighborhood and offering examples of the many influences surrounding her. Esperanza quickly befriends Lucy and Rachel Guerrero, two Texan girls who live across the street. Lucy,

Rachel, Esperanza, and Esperanza's little sister, Nenny, have many adventures in the small space of their neighborhood. As the vignettes progress, the novel depicts Esperanza's budding personal maturity and developing world outlook. Esperanza then meets a person named Meme Ortiz, and they become fast friends, each participating in The Tarzan Tree Jumping Contest, an annual event in which Meme Ortiz breaks his arms. Esperanza later slips into puberty and likes it when a boy watches her dance at a baptism party. Esperanza's newfound views lead her to become friends with Sally, a girl her age who wears black nylon stockings, makeup, high heels, and short skirts, and uses boys as an escape from her abusive father. Sally, a beautiful girl according to her father, can get into trouble with being as beautiful as she is. Esperanza is not completely comfortable with Sally's sexuality. Their friendship is compromised when Sally ditches Esperanza for a boy at a carnival. As a result, Esperanza is sexually assaulted by a man at the carnival. Earlier at her first job, an elderly man tricked her into kissing him on the lips. Esperanza's traumatic experiences and observations of the women in her neighborhood cement her desire to escape Mango Street. She later realizes that she will never fully be able to leave Mango Street behind. She vows that after she leaves she will return to help the people she has left behind. Esperanza exclaims that Mango Street does not hold her in both arms; instead, which sets her free (*adapted from Wikipedia*).

anemic

know by heart   Sister Superior

get hollered at   boulevard

holy pictures   ragged

1   The special kids, the ones who wear keys around their necks, get to eat in the canteen. The canteen! Even the name sounds important. And these kids at lunch time go there because their mothers aren't home or home is too far away to get to.

My home isn't far but it's not close either, and somehow I got it in my head one day to ask my mother to make me a sandwich and write a note to the principal so I could eat in the canteen, too.

Oh no, she says pointing the butter knife at me as if I'm starting trouble, no sir. Next thing you know everybody will be wanting a bag lunch-I'll be up all night cutting bread into little triangles, this one with mayonnaise, this one with mustard, no pickles on mine, but mustard on one side please. You kids just like to invent more work for me.

2 But Nenny[1] says she doesn't want to eat at school-ever-because she likes to go home with her best friend Gloria who lives across the schoolyard. Gloria's mama has a big color T.V. and all they do is watch cartoons. Kiki and Carlos,[2] on the other hand, are patrol boys. They don't want to eat at school, either. They like to stand out in the cold especially if it's raining. They think suffering is good for you ever since they say that movie "300 Spartans".

I'm no Spartan and hold up an anemic wrist to prove it. I can't even blow up a balloon without getting dizzy. And besides, I know how to make my own lunch. If I ate at school there'd be less dishes to wash. You would see me less and less and like me better. Everyday at noon my chair would be empty. Where is my favorite daughter you would cry, and when I came home finally at 3 p.m. you would appreciate me.[3]

Okay, okay, my mother says after three days of this. And the following morning I get to go to school with my mother's letter and a rice sandwich because we don't have lunch meat.

3 Mondays or Fridays, it doesn't matter, mornings always go by slow and this day especially. But lunch time came finally

---

1) The narrator's elder sister.
2) The narrator's elder brothers.
3) 전체적으로 가정법임에 유의. 도시락을 싸가지고 갈 경우를 가정한 표현들.

and I got to get in line with the stay-at-school kids. Everything is fine until the nun who knows all the canteen kids by heart looks at me and says: you, who sent you here? And since I am shy, I don't say anything, just hold out my hand with the letter. This is no good, she says, till Sister Superior gives the okay. Go upstairs and see her. And so I went.

I had to wait for two kids in front of me to get hollered at, one because he did something in class, the other because he didn't. My turn came and I stood in front of the big desk with holy pictures under the glass while the Sister Superior read my letter. It went like this;

> Dear Sister Superior, Please let Esperanza eat in the lunch room because she lives too far away and she gets tired. As you can see she is very skinny. I hope to God she does not faint. Thanking you, Mrs. E. Cordero.

You don't live far, she says. You live across the boulevard. That's only four blocks. Not even. Three maybe. Three long blocks away from here. I bet I can see your house from my window. Which one? Come here. Which one is your house?

And then she made me stand up on a box of books and point. That one? She said pointing to a row of ugly 3 flats,[4] the ones

---

4) 보기 싫은 아파트 3채가 나란히 줄지어 서 있는 것.

even the raggedy men are ashamed to go into. Yes, I nodded even though I knew that wasn't my house and started to cry. I always cry when nuns yell at me, even if they're not yelling.

Then she was sorry and said I could stay ____ just for today, not tomorrow or the day after ____ you go home. And I said yes and could I please have a Kleenex ____ I had to blow my nose.

In the canteen, which was nothing special, lots of boys and girls watched while I cried and ate my sandwich, the bread already greasy and the rice cold.

1. Why does Esperanza want to eat in the canteen? (section 1)

2. Why does the mother reject Esperanza's request of a lunch bag at first? (section 1)

3. How does Esperanza convince her mother to get her lunch and write the permission note? (section 2)

4. Why does she take a rice sandwich instead of a meat one? (section 2)

5. Why does Esperanza fail in eating in the canteen? (section 3)

6. Why does she go and see Sister Superior? (section 3)

7. How does Sister Superior respond to the mother's note? (section 3)

8. Why does Esperanza give affirmation to Sister Superior's pointing her house even if it is not actually hers? (section 3)

The First Job

Sandra Cisneros

Vocabulary	
dime store	night shift
hotdog stand	punch the time clock
open water hydrant	oriental man
negative strip	

1 It wasn't as if I didn't want to work. I did. I had even gone to the social security office[1] the month before to get my social security number. I needed money. The Catholic high school cost a lot, and papa said nobody went to public school unless you wanted to turn out bad.

I thought I'd find an easy job, the kind other kids had, working in the dime store or maybe a hotdog stand. And though I hadn't started looking yet, I thought I might the week after next. But when I came home that afternoon, all wet

---

1) 한국의 주민등록번호와 비슷한 개념의 social security number를 발행해 주는 곳. 이 번호가 있어야 취업을 할 수 있는 정식 시민으로 간주됨.

because Tito had pushed me into the open water hydrant ___ only I had sort of let him ___ Mama called me in the kitchen before I could even go and change, and Aunt Lala was sitting there drinking her coffee with a spoon. Aunt Lala said she had found a job for me at the Per Pan Photo Finishers on North Braodway where she worked, and how old was I, and to show up tomorrow saying I was one year older, and that was that.[2]

2   So the next morning I put on the navy blue dress that made me look older and borrowed money for lunch and bus fare because Aunt Lala said I wouldn't get paid till the next Friday, and I went in and saw the boss of the Peter Pan Photo Finishers on North Braodway where Aunt Lala worked and lied about my age like she told me to and sure enough, I started that same day.

In my job I had to wear white gloves. I was supposed to match negatives with their prints, just look at the picture and look for the same one on the negative strip, put it in the envelope, and do the next one. That's all. I didn't know where these envelopes were coming from or where they were going. I just did what I was told.

It was real easy, and I guess I wouldn't have minded it except

---

2) 내가 몇 살인지 물어보고는 한 살 더 올려서 말하라고 하면서 내일 출근해 보라고 함. 일이 그렇게 되었음.

that you got tired after a while and I didn't know if I could sit down or not, and then I started sitting down only when the two ladies next to me did. After a while they started to laugh and came up to me and said I could sit when I wanted to, and I said I knew.

When lunchtime came, I was scared to eat alone in the company lunchroom with all those men and ladies looking, so I ate real fast standing in one of the washroom stalls and had lots of time left over, so I went back to work early. But then break time came, and not knowing where else to go, I went into the coatroom because there was a bench there.

3 I guess it was the time for the night shift or middle shift to arrive because a few people came in and punched the time clock, and an older Oriental man said hello and we talked for a while about my just starting, and he said we could be friends and next time to go in the lunchroom and sit with him, and I felt better. He had nice eyes and I didn't fell so nervous anymore. Then he asked if I knew what day it was, and when I said I didn't, he said it was his birthday and would I please give him a birthday kiss. I thought I would because he was so old and just as I was about to put my lips on his cheek, he grabs my face with both hands and kisses me hard on the mouth and doesn't let go.

Comprehension Check-Up Questions

1. Why does the narrator take job rather than go to the high school? (section 1)

2. How is the narrator's first day at work? (section 2)

3. What shocks the narrator so much at the ending? (section 3)

Eleven

Sandra Cisneros

Woman Hollering Creek and Other Stories that includes "Eleven" is a book of short stories published in 1991 by Sandra Cisneros. The collection reflects Cisneros's experience of being surrounded by American influences while still being familially bound to her Mexican heritage as she grew up north of the Mexico–US border. These tales focus on the social role of women, and their relationships with the men and other women in their lives. The vignettes are quite short on average; the longest is 29 pages, while the shortest is fewer than five paragraphs. Despite such limited space, Cisneros experiments with daring poetic prose in her storytelling; for example, each story presents a new character with a distinct literary voice and style(*adapted from Wikipedia*).

Vocabulary

coatroom	alley
parking meter	shove
bunch up into a little ball	tippy-tip

1   What they don't understand about birthdays and what they never tell you is that when you're eleven, you're also ten, and nine, and eight, and seven, and six, and five, and four, and three, and two, and one. And when you wake up on your eleventh birthday you expect to feel eleven, but you don't. You open your eyes and everything's just like yesterday, only it's today. And you don't feel eleven at all. You feel like you're still ten. And you are ____ underneath the year that makes you eleven. Like some days you might say something stupid, and that's the part of you that's still ten. Or maybe some days you might need to sit on your mama's lap because you're scared, and that's the part of you that's five. And maybe one day when you're all grown up maybe you will need to cry like if you're three, and that's okay. That's what I tell Mama when she's sad and needs to cry. Maybe she's feeling three. Because the way you grow old is kind of like an onion or like the rings inside a tree trunk or like my little wooden dolls that fit one inside the other, each year inside the next one. That's how being eleven years old is.

You don't feel eleven. Not right away. It takes a few days, weeks even, sometimes even months before you say Eleven when they ask you. And you don't feel smart eleven, not until you're almost twelve. That's the way it is.

2   Only today I wish I didn't have only eleven years rattling inside me like pennies in a tin Band-Aid box. Today I wish I was one hundred and two instead of eleven because if I was one hundred and two I'd have known what to say when Mrs. Price put the red sweater on my desk. I would've known how to tell her it wasn't mine instead of just sitting there with that look on my face and nothing coming out of my mouth.

"Whose is this?" Mrs. Price says, and she holds the red sweater up in the air for all the class to see. "Whose! It's been sitting in the coatroom for a month."

"Not mine." says everybody. "Not me."

"It has to belong to somebody." Mrs. Price keeps saying, but nobody can remember. It's an ugly sweater with red plastic buttons and a collar and sleeves all stretched out like you could use it for a jump rope. It's maybe a thousand years old and even if it belonged to me I wouldn't say so.

Maybe because I'm skinny, maybe because she doesn't like me, that stupid Sylvia Saldivar says, "I think it belongs to Rachel." an ugly sweater like that, all ragged and old, but Mrs. Price believes her. Mrs. Price takes the sweater and puts it right on my desk, but when I open my mouth nothing comes out.

"That's not, I don't, you're not . . . Not mine." I finally say in a little voice that was maybe me when I was four.

"Of course, it's yours." Mrs. Price says. "I remember you

wearing it once." Because she's older and the teacher, she's right and I'm not.

Not mine, not mine, not mine, but Mrs. Price is already turning to page thirty-two, and math problem number four[1]. I don't know why but all of a sudden I'm feeling sick inside, like the part of me that's there[2] wants to come out of my eyes, only I squeeze them shut tight and bite down on my teeth real hard and try to remember today I am eleven, eleven. Mama is making a cake for me for tonight, and when Papa comes home everybody will sing Happy birthday, happy birthday to you.

But when the sick feeling goes away and I open my eyes, the red sweater's still sitting there like a big red mountain. I move the red sweater to the corner of my desk with my ruler. I move my pencil and books and eraser as far from it as possible. I even move my chair a little to the right. Not mine, not mine, not mine.

In my head I'm thinking how long till luncheon time, how long till I can take the red sweater and throw it over the schoolyard fence, or leave it hanging on a parking meter, or bunch it up into a little ball and toss it in the alley.[3] Except when math period ends Mrs. Price says loud and in front of everybody,[4]

---

1) 내 것이 아니다 라고 수차례 (마음속으로) 외쳤으나 선생님은 (듣지 않고) 벌써 36페이지를 펴서 는 수학 문제 4번을 풀고 있음.

2) 내 안에 있는 나의 일부가

3) 작은 공으로 돌돌 뭉쳐 복도에서 던지고 놀다.

"Now, Rachel, That's enough." because she sees I've shoved the red sweater to the tippy-tip corner of my desk and it's hanging all over the edge like a waterfall, but I don't care.

"Rachel." Mrs. Price says. She says it like she's getting mad. "You put that sweater on right now and no more nonsense."

"But it's not ____"

"Now!" Mrs. Price says.

This is when I wish I wasn't eleven, because all the years inside of me ____ ten, nine, eight, seven, six, five, four, three, two, and one ____ are pushing at the back of my eyes when I put one arm through one sleeve of the sweater that smells like cottage cheese, and then the other arm through the other and stand there with my arms apart like if the sweater hurts me and it does, all itchy and full of germs that aren't even mine.

That's when everything I've been holding in since this morning, since when Mrs. Price put the sweater on my desk, finally lets go, and all of a sudden I'm crying in front of everybody. I wish I was invisible but I'm not. I'm eleven and it's my birthday today and I'm crying like I'm three in front of everybody. I put my head down on the desk and bury my face in my stupid clown-sweater arms. My face all hot and spit coming out of my mouth because I can't stop the little animal noises from coming out of me, until there aren't any more

---

4) 이 문장은 앞 문장과 연결, 한 문장으로 이해. Except = but.

tears left in my eyes, and it's just my body shaking like when you have the hiccups, and my whole head hurts like when you drink milk too fast.

3 But the worst part is right before the bell rings for lunch. That stupid Phyllis Lopez, who is even dumber than Sylvia Saldivar, says she remembers the red sweater is hers! I take it off right away and give it to her, only Mrs. Price pretends like everything's okay.

Today I'm eleven. There's a cake Mama's making for tonight, and when Papa comes home from work we'll eat it. There'll be candles and presents and everybody will sing Happy birthday, happy birthday to you, Rachel, only it's too late.

I'm eleven today. I'm eleven, ten, nine, eight, seven, six, five, four, three, two, and one, but I wish I was one hundred and two. I wish I was anything but eleven, because I want today to be far away already, far away like a runaway balloon, like a tiny *o* in the sky, so tiny-tiny you have to close your eyes to see it. (from *Woman Hollering Creek*)

By Any Other Name

Santha Rama Rau

Santha Rama Rau (1923–2009) was born the daughter of Sir Benegal Rama Rau, an Indian public servant, and his wife Dhanvanthi Rama Rau, an early advocate of Planned Parenthood. Santha's father was a member of the elite and prestigious Indian Civil Service, and he held the longest ever tenure (1949–1957) as Governor of the Reserve Bank of India. Santha's paternal family was highly distinguished. Her grandfather, Benegal Raghavendra Rau, had been one of the earliest Indian doctors educated in western medicine. Her father's elder brother, Benegal Narsing Rau, was a renowned civil servant, jurist and statesman who had had an important role in drafting the Constitution of India. Another uncle, Benegal Shiva Rao, was an eminent journalist and member of Parliament. In her early years, Rama Rau lived in an India under British rule, one incident of which was recounted in her short memoir entitled "By Any Other Name". Around 1929, she accompanied her father on a political trip to England. There she was educated at St Paul's Girls' School, and left in 1939. After short traveling through South Africa, she returned to India to discover a different place than she remembered. She applied to Wellesley College, Wellesley, Massachusetts, in the United States, and was the first Indian student to be accepted there. She graduated with honors in 1944. Shortly afterward, she published her first book *Home to India.*

"By Any Other Name" is a story taken from the author's autobiography, *Gifts of Passage.* Santha Rama Rau lived in an India under British rule. When aged 5 and a half, with her 8-year-old sister Premila, she briefly attended an Anglo-Indian School where the teacher anglicized their names. Santha's name was changed to Cynthia and her sister's was changed to Pamela. The environment there they found to be condescending, as their teacher told them that "Indians cheat". They walked home, and never returned to that school. The incident was recounted in Rama Rau's short memoir entitled "By Any Other Name".

Vocabulary	
headmistress's study	braids
intimidated	palpitating
inspection tours	siesta
headquarters	ayah
postmonsoon	courtesy
procession	a tiring walk
insular	deserted

1   At the Anglo-Indian day school in Zorinabad to which my sister and I were sent when she was eight and I was five and a half, they changed our names. On the first day of school, a hot, windless morning of a north Indian September, we stood in the headmistress's study and she said, "Now you're the new girls.

What are your names?"

My sister answered for us. "I am Premila, and she" ____ nodding in my direction ____ "is Santha."

The headmistress had been in India, I suppose, fifteen years or so, but she still smiled her helpless inability to cope with Indian names.[1] Her rimless half-glasses glittered, and the precarious bun[2] on the top of her head trembled as she shook her head. "Oh, my dears, those are much too hard for me. Suppose we give you pretty English names. Wouldn't that be more jolly? Let's see, now ____ Pamela for you, I think." She shrugged in a baffled way at my sister. "That's as close as I can get. And for you." she said to me, "how about Cynthia? Isn't that nice?"

My sister was always less easily intimidated than I was[3] and, while she kept a stubborn silence,[4] I said, "Thank you." in a very tiny voice.

2 We had been sent to that school because my father, among responsibilities as an officer of the civil service,[5] had

---

1) she still smiled her helpless inability to cope with Indian names. 인도이름을 제대로 발음할 수 없음을 웃음으로 얼버무리다. cope with 극복하다, 대처하다.

2) precarious bun 위험스럽게 얹힌 머리 (둥근) 다발.

3) My sister was always less easily intimidated than I was. 언니는 늘 나보다 (협박 등에) 잘 안 넘어가는 사람이었다.

4) stubborn silence 완고한 침묵. 절대 말 안하고 있음.

5) an officer of the civil service 공무원.

a tour of duty to perform in the villages around that steamy little provincial town, where he had his headquarters at that time.6) He used to make his shorter inspection tours on horseback, and a week before, in the stale heat of a typically postmonsoon day we had waved good-by to him and a little procession ____ an assistant, a secretary, two bearers, and the man to look after the bedding rolls and luggage. They rode away through our large garden, still bright green from the rains, and we turned back into the twilight of the house and the sound of fans whispering in every room.

Up to then, my mother had refused to send Premila to school in the British-run establishments7) of that time, because, she used to say "you can bury a dog's tail for seven years and it still comes out curly; and you can take a Britisher away from his home for a lifetime and he still remains insular". The question probably never would have come up if Mother's health had not broken down. For the first time in my life, she was not able to continue the lessons she had been giving us every morning. So our Hindi books were put away and we were sent to the Anglo-Indian school.

---

6) the villages around that steamy little provincial town, where he had his headquarters at that time. 그 무더운 작은 지방 소도시 — 거기에 아버지는 그 때 당시 자신의 본부를 가지고 있었다 — 주위의 마을들.
7) British-run establishments 영국인들이 운영하는 (교육)기관.

though it were swallowing several times quickly. The lessons were mostly concerned with reading and writing and simple numbers ____ things that my mother had already taught me ____ and I paid very little attention. The teacher wrote on the easel blackboard words like "bat" and "cat", which seemed babyish to me; only "apple" was new and incomprehensible.

When it was time for the lunch recess,13) I followed the girl with braids out onto the veranda. There the children from the other classes were assembled. I saw Premila at once and ran over to her as she had charge of our lunchbox. The children were all opening packages and sitting down to eat sandwiches. Premila and I were the only ones who had Indian food ____ thin wheat chapatties,14) some vegetable curry, and a bottle of buttermilk. Premila thrust half of it into my hand and whispered fiercely that I should go and sit with my class, because that was what the others seemed to be doing.

The enormous black eyes of the little Indian girl from my class looked at my food longingly so I offered her some. But she only shook her head and plowed her way solemnly through her sandwiches.15)

---

13) lunch recess 점심 (쉬는) 시간
14) chapatties. a type of flat, round Indian bread.
15) plow her way solemnly through her sandwiches 음울하게 자기 샌드위치를 천천히 먹었다. plow (one's way) through sth. to make slow progress through sth difficult or boring. ex. plow her way through the book.

I was very sleepy after lunch, because at home we always took a siesta. It was usually a pleasant time of day, with the bedroom darkened against the harsh afternoon sun, the drifting off into sleep with the sound of Mother's voice reading a story in one's mind, and, finally the shrill, fussy voice of the ayah waking one for tea.

5 At school, we rested for a short time, and then we were expected to play games. During the hot part of the afternoon we played indoors, and after the shadows had begun to lengthen and the slight breeze of the evening had come up we moved outside to the wide courtyard.

I had never really grasped the system of competitive games. At home, whenever we played tag or guessing games,16) I was always allowed to "win . . . because", Mother used to tell Premila, "she is the youngest, and we have to allow for that." I had often heard her say it, and it seemed quite reasonable to me, but the result was that I had no clear idea of what "winning" meant.

When we played twos-and-threes that afternoon at school, in accordance with my training,17) I let one of the small English boys catch me, but was naturally rather puzzled when the other

---

16) tag or guessing games 말 잇기 놀이나 스무고개.
17) in accordance with my training (집에서) 훈련받은 것에 맞추어. 교육받은 대로.

children did not return the courtesy. I ran about for what seemed like hours without ever catching anyone, until it was time for school to close. Much later I learned that my attitude was called "not being a good sport", and I stopped allowing to be caught, but it was not for years that I really learned the spirit of the thing.

6 When I saw our car come up to the school gate, I broke away from my classmates and rushed toward it yelling, "Ayah! Ayah!" It seemed like an eternity since I had seen her that morning ___ a wizened, affectionate figure in her white cotton sari, giving me dozens of urgent and useless instruction on how to be a good girl at school. Premila followed more sedately and she told me on the way home never to do that again in front of the other children.

When we got home we went straight to Mother's high, white room to have tea with her, and I immediately climbed onto the bed and bounced gently up and down on the springs. Mother asked how we had liked our first day in school. I was so pleased to be home and to have left that peculiar Cynthia behind. I had nothing whatever to say about school, except to ask what "apple" meant. But Premila told Mother about the classes, and added that in her class they had weekly tests to see if they had learned their lessons well.

I asked, "What's a test?"

Premila said, "You're too small to have them. You won't have them in your class for donkey's years." She had learned the expression that day and was using it for the first time. We all laughed enormously at her wit. She also told Mother, in an aside, that we should take sandwiches to school the next day. Not, she said, that she minded. But they would be simpler for me to handle.

That whole lovely evening I didn't think about school at all. I sprinted barefoot across the lawns with my favorite playmate, the cook's son, to the stream at the end of the garden. We quarreled in our usual way, and waited for the night to bring out the smell of the jasmine. I listened with fascination to his stories of ghosts and demons, until I was too frightened to cross the garden alone in the semidarkness. The ayah found me, shouted at the cook's son, scolded me, hurried me in to supper ____ it was an entirely usual, wonderful evening.

7   It was a week after the day of Premila's first test, that our lives changed rather abruptly. I was sitting at the back of class, in my usual inattentive way, only half listening to the teacher. I had started a rather guarded friendship with the girl with the braids, whose name turned out to be Nalini (Nancy, in school). The three other Indian children were already fast

friends. Even at that age it was apparent to all of us that friendship with the English or Anglo-Indian children was out of the question. Occasionally during the class, my new friend and I would draw pictures and show them to each other secretly.

The door opened sharply and Premila marched in. At first, the teacher smiled at her in a kindly and encouraging way and said, "Now, you're little Cynthia's sister?" Premila didn't even look at her. She stood with her feet planted firmly apart and her shoulders rigid, and addressed herself directly to me. "Get up." she said. "We're going home."

I didn't know what had happened, but I was aware that it was a crisis of some sort. I rose obediently and started to walk toward my sister.

"Bring your pencils and your notebook." she said.

I went back for them, and together we left the room. The teacher started to say something just as Premila closed the door, but we didn't wait to hear what it was.

In complete silence we left the school grounds and started to walk home. Then I asked Premila what the matter was. All she would say was "We're going home for good."[18]

8   It was a very tiring walk for a child of five and a half, and I dragged along behind Premila with my pencils growing

---

18) for good 영원히.

sticky in my hand. I can still remember looking at the dusty hedges,[19] and the tangles of thorns[20] in the ditches by the side of the road, smelling the faint fragrance from the eucalyptus trees and wondering whether we would ever reach home. Occasionally a horse-drawn tonga[21] passed us, and the women, in their pink or green silks, stared at Premila and me trudging along on the side of the road. A few coolies[22] and a line of women carrying baskets of vegetables on their heads smiled at us. But it was nearing the hottest time of day, and the road was almost deserted. I walked more and more slowly and shouted to Premila, from time to time, "Wait for me!" She spoke to me only once, and that was to tell me to carry my notebook on my head, because of the sun.

When we got to our house the ayah was just taking a tray of lunch into Mother's room. She immediately started a long, worried questioning about what are you children doing back here at this hour of the day. Mother looked very startled and very concerned,[23] and asked what had happened.

Premila said, "We had our test today, and she made me and

---

19) dusty hedges 먼지가 가득 앉은 (길가의) 키 작은 나무들.
20) the tangles of thorns 가시나무 덤불들.
21) horse-drawn tonga 말이 끄는 인력거.
22) coolie 뜨내기 일꾼들.
23) Mother looked very startled and very concerned. 어머니는 매우 당황스럽고 걱정스런 표정이었다.

the other Indians sit at the back of the room, with a desk between each one."

Mother said, "Why was that, darling?"

"She said it was because Indians cheat." Premila added. "So don't think we should go back to that school."

Mother looked very distant,24) and was silent a long time. At last she said, "Of course not, darling." She sounded displeased.

We all shared the curry she was having for lunch, and afterward I was sent off to the beautifully familiar bedroom for my siesta.25) I could hear Mother and Premila talking through the open door.

Mother said, "Do you suppose she understood all that?"

Premila said, "I shouldn't think so. She's a baby."

Mother said, "Well, I hope it won't bother her."

Of course, they were both wrong. I understood it perfectly and I remember it all very clearly. But I put it happily away, because it had all happened to a girl called Cynthia, and I never was really particularly interested in her.

---

24) looked very distant 생각에 사로잡힌 듯 했다. distant는 생각(꿈) 따위로 마음이 먼 곳에 가 있는.

Comprehension Check-Up Questions

1. How old were Premila and Santha when the story happened? (section 1)

2. What English names did the headmistress give to them? (section 1)

3. How did they respond when the headmistress gave them the new English names? (section 1)

4. What did Santha's father do? (section 2)

5. Why did her mother refuse to send the children to a British-run school? (section 2)

6. Why did she change her mind? (section 2)

7. In what respects was the school different from general Indian architecture? (section 3)

8. How many Indian and British children were there? (section 3)

9. Where in the classroom were Indian children sitting? What clothing and accessory did the Indian girl next to Santha? (section 3)

10. How difficult was the class for Santha? (section 4)

11. What did the most children take for the lunch and how about Santha? (section 4)

12. Why did Santha feel so sleepy after lunch? How had siesta been at home? (section 4)

13. What did children do after lunch recess? (section 5)

14. What of the game most embarrassed Santha? (section 5)

15. How did Santha feel when the school was over? (section 6)

16. How did Santha spend that afternoon and evening and how did she feel about it? (section 6)

Harrison Bergeron

Kurt Vonnegut

Kurt Vonnegut Jr. (/ˈvɒnəɡət/;1922-2007) was an American writer. In a career spanning over 50 years, Vonnegut published 14 novels, three short story collections, five plays, and five works of non-fiction, with further collections being published after his death. He is most famous for his darkly satirical, best-selling novel *Slaughterhouse-Five* (1969). Born and raised in Indianapolis, Indiana, Vonnegut attended Cornell University but dropped out in January 1943 and enlisted in the United States Army. As part of his training, he studied mechanical engineering at Carnegie Institute of Technology (now Carnegie Mellon University) and the University of Tennessee. He was then deployed to Europe to fight in World War II and was captured by the Germans during the Battle of the Bulge. He was interned in Dresden and survived the Allied bombing of the city by taking refuge in a meat locker of the slaughterhouse where he was imprisoned. After the war, Vonnegut married Jane Marie Cox, with whom he had three children. He later adopted his sister's three sons, after she died of cancer and her husband was killed in a train accident. Vonnegut published his first novel, *Player Piano*, in 1952. The novel was reviewed positively but was not commercially successful. In the nearly 20 years that followed, Vonnegut published several novels that were only marginally successful, such as *Cat's Cradle* (1963) and *God Bless You, Mr. Rosewater* (1964). Vonnegut's breakthrough was his commercially and critically successful sixth novel, *Slaughterhouse-Five*. The book's anti-war sentiment resonated with its readers amidst the ongoing Vietnam War and its reviews were generally positive. After its release, *Slaughterhouse-Five* went to the top of *The New York Times Best Seller list*, thrusting Vonnegut into fame. He was invited to give speeches, lectures and commencement addresses around the country and received many awards and honors.

"**Harrison Bergeron**" is a satirical and dystopian science-fiction short story, first published in October 1961. Originally published in *The Magazine of Fantasy and Science Fiction,* the story was republished in the author's *Welcome to the Monkey House* collection in 1968. The story received the 2019 Hall of Fame Award from the Libertarian Futurist Society. The story describes the imaginary society of America in 2081. In the year 2081, the 211th, 212th, and 213th amendments to the Constitution dictate that all Americans are fully equal and not allowed to be smarter, better-looking, or more physically able than anyone else. The Handicapper General's agents enforce the equality laws, forcing citizens.

amendment

constitution

unceasing vigilance

drove people crazy

obscene

toying with

vague notion

wince

ball peen hammer

'em

better'ntwenty-one-gun salute

temples

wore out

bargain: don't call that a bargain

reckon

impediment

hideous

luminous

grackle squawk

suspicion of plotting

overthrow

full length

calibrated

wavy lenses

semmetry

junkyard

consternation

crippled, hobbled, sickened

padlock

cowering people

barons and dukes and earls

batons

blackout

doozy

1   The year was 2081, and everybody was finally equal. They weren't only equal before God and the law. They were equal every which way. Nobody was smarter than anybody else. Nobody was better looking than anybody else. Nobody was stronger or quicker than anybody else. All this equality was due to the 211th, 212th, and 213th Amendments to the Constitution, and to the unceasing vigilance of agents of the United States Handicapper General.

Some things about living still weren't quite right, though. April, for instance, still drove people crazy. And it was in that clammy month that the H-G men took George and Hazel Bergeron's fourteen-year-old son, Harrison, away.

It was tragic, but George and Hazel couldn't think about it very hard. Hazel had a perfectly average intelligence, which meant she couldn't think about anything except in short bursts. And George, while his intelligence was way above normal, had a little mental handicap radio in his ear. He was required by law to wear it at all times. It was tuned to a government transmitter. Every twenty seconds or so, the transmitter would send out some sharp noise to keep people like George from taking unfair advantage of their brains.

2   George and Hazel were watching television. There were tears on Hazel's cheeks, but she'd forgotten for the moment what they were about.

On the television screen were ballerinas.

A buzzer sounded in George's head. His thoughts fled in panic, like bandits from a burglar alarm.

"That was a real pretty dance, that dance they just did." said Hazel.

"Huh?" said George.

"That dance ___ it was nice." said Hazel.

"Yup." said George. He tried to think a little about the ballerinas. They weren't really very good ___ no better than anybody else would have been, anyway. They were burdened with sashweights and bags of birdshot, and their faces were masked, so that no one, seeing a free and graceful gesture or a pretty face, would feel like something obscene. George was toying with the vague notion that maybe dancers shouldn't be handicapped. But he didn't get very far with it before another noise in his ear radio scattered his thoughts.

George winced. So did two out of the eight ballerinas.

Hazel saw him wince. Having no mental handicap herself she had to ask George what the latest sound had been.

"Sounded like somebody hitting a milk bottle with a ball peen hammer." said George.

"I'd think it would be real interesting, hearing all the different sounds." said Hazel, a little envious. "All the things they think up."

"Um." said George.

"Only, if I was Handicapper General, you know what I would do?" said Hazel. Hazel, as a matter of fact, bore a strong resemblance to the Handicapper General, a woman named Diana Moon Glampers. "If I was Diana Moon Glampers" said Hazel, "I'd have chimes on Sunday ___ just chimes. Kind of in honor of religion."

"I could think, if it was just chimes." said George.

"Well ___ maybe make 'em real loud." said Hazel. "I think I'd make a good Handicapper General."

"Good as anybody else." said George.

"Who knows better'n I do what normal is?" said Hazel.

"Right." said George. He began to think glimmeringly about his abnormal son who was now in jail, about Harrison, but a twenty-one-gun salute in his head stopped that.

"Boy!" said Hazel, "that was a doozy, wasn't it?"

It was such a doozy that George was white and trembling and tears stood on the rims of his red eyes. Two of the eight ballerinas had collapsed to the studio floor, were holding their temples.

3   "All of a sudden you look so tired." said Hazel. "Why don't you stretch out on the sofa, so you can rest your handicap bag on the pillows, honeybunch." She was referring to the forty-seven

pounds of birdshot in canvas bag, which was padlocked around George's neck. "Go on and rest the bag for a little while." she said. "I don't care if you're not equal to me for a while."

George weighed the bag with his hands. "I don't mind it." he said. "I don't notice it any more. It's just a part of me."

"You been so tired lately ___ kind of wore out." said Hazel. "If there was just some way we could make a little hole in the bottom of the bag, and just take out a few of them lead balls. Just a few."

"Two years in prison and two thousand dollars fine for every ball I took out." said George. "I don't call that a bargain."

"If you could just take a few out when you came home from work" said Hazel. "I mean ___ you don't compete with anybody around here. You just set around."

"If I tried to get away with it" said George, "then other people'd get away with it and pretty soon we'd be right back to the dark ages again, with everybody competing against everybody else. You wouldn't like that, would you?"

"I'd hate it." said Hazel.

"There you are." said George. "The minute[1] people start cheating on laws, what do you think happens to society?"

If Hazel hadn't been able to come up with an answer to this question, George couldn't have supplied one. A siren was going

---

1) The minute : The moment : As soon as

off in his head.

"Reckon it'd fall all apart." said Hazel.

"What would?" said George blankly.

"Society." said Hazel uncertainly. "Wasn't that what you just said?"

"Who knows?" said George.

4　The television program was suddenly interrupted for a news bulletin.[2] It wasn't clear at first as to what the bulletin was about, since the announcer, like all announcers, had a serious speech impediment. For about half a minute, and in a state of high excitement, the announcer tried to say, "Ladies and gentlemen."

He finally gave up, handed the bulletin to a ballerina to read.

"That's all right ___" Hazel said of the announcer, "he tried. That's the big thing. He tried to do the best he could with what God gave him. He should get a nice raise[3] for trying so hard."

"Ladies and gentlemen." said the ballerina, reading the bulletin. She must have been extraordinarily beautiful, because the mask she wore was hideous. And it was easy to see that she was the strongest and most graceful of all the dancers, for her handicap bags were as big as those worn by two-hundred-pound men.

---

2) news bulletin. 뉴스 속보.
3) raise. 봉급 인상.

And she had to apologize at once for her voice, which was a very unfair voice for a woman to use. Her voice was a warm, luminous, timeless melody. "Excuse me ____ " she said, and she began again, making her voice absolutely uncompetitive.

"Harrison Bergeron, age fourteen." she said in a grackle squawk, "has just escaped from jail, where he was held on suspicion of plotting to overthrow the government. He is a genius and an athlete, is under-handicapped, and should be regarded as extremely dangerous."

A police photograph of Harrison Bergeron was flashed on the screen ____ upside down, then sideways, upside down again, then right side up.[4] The picture showed the full length of Harrison against a background calibrated in feet and inches. He was exactly seven feet tall.

The rest of Harrison's appearance was Halloween and hardware[5]. Nobody had ever worn heavier handicaps. He had outgrown hindrances faster than the H-G men could think them up. Instead of a little ear radio for a mental handicap, he wore a tremendous pair of earphones, and spectacles with thick wavy lenses. The spectacles were intended to make him not only half blind, but to give him whanging headaches besides.

---

4) 방송국 기사도 "normal"하기 때문에 서툴게 자료를 다루고 있음.
5) Halloween and hardware. 핸디캡 장치를 하도 많이 달고 있어서 모습이 할로윈 분장한 사람이나 철물점처럼 되어버렸음.

Scrap metal was hung all over him. Ordinarily, there was a certain symmetry, a military neatness to the handicaps issued to strong people, but Harrison looked like a walking junkyard. In the race of life, Harrison carried three hundred pounds.

And to offset his good looks, the H-G men required that he wear at all times a red rubber ball for a nose, keep his eyebrows shaved off, and cover his even white teeth with black caps at snaggle-tooth random.

"If you see this boy." said the ballerina, "do not ____ I repeat, do not-try to reason with him."

5   There was the shriek of a door being torn from its hinges.

Screams and barking cries of consternation came from the television set. The photograph of Harrison Bergeron on the screen jumped again and again, as though dancing to the tune of an earthquake.

George Bergeron correctly identified the earthquake, and well he might have ____ for many was the time his own home had danced to the same crashing tune. "My God ___" said George, "that must be Harrison!"

The realization was blasted from his mind instantly by the sound of an automobile collision in his head.

When George could open his eyes again, the photograph of Harrison was gone. A living, breathing Harrison filled the screen.

Clanking, clownish, and huge, Harrison stood in the center of the studio. The knob of the uprooted studio door was still in his hand. Ballerinas, technicians, musicians, and announcers cowered on their knees before him, expecting to die.

"I am the Emperor!" cried Harrison. "Do you hear? I am the Emperor! Everybody must do what I say at once!" He stamped his foot and the studio shook.

"Even as I stand here ____" he bellowed, "crippled, hobbled, sickened ____ I am a greater ruler than any man who ever lived! Now watch me become what I can become!"

Harrison tore the straps of his handicap harness like wet tissue paper, tore straps guaranteed to support five thousand pounds.

Harrison's scrap-iron handicaps crashed to the floor.

Harrison thrust his thumbs under the bar of the padlock that secured his head harness. The bar snapped like celery. Harrison smashed his headphones and spectacles against the wall.

He flung away his rubber-ball nose, revealed a man that would have awed Thor, the god of thunder.

"I shall now select my Empress!" he said, looking down on the cowering people. "Let the first woman who dares rise to her feet claim her mate and her throne!"

A moment passed, and then a ballerina arose, swaying like a willow.

Harrison plucked the mental handicap from her ear, snapped

off her physical handicaps with marvelous delicacy. Last of all, he removed her mask.

She was blindingly beautiful.

"Now." said Harrison, taking her hand, "shall we show the people the meaning of the word dance? Music!" he commanded.

The musicians scrambled back into their chairs, and Harrison stripped them of their handicaps, too. "Play your best." he told them, "and I'll make you barons and dukes and earls."

The music began. It was normal at first ____ cheap, silly, false. But Harrison snatched two musicians from their chairs, waved them like batons as he sang the music as he wanted it played. He slammed them back into their chairs.

The music began again and was much improved.

Harrison and his Empress merely listened to the music for a while ____ listened gravely, as though synchronizing their heartbeats with it.

They shifted their weights to their toes.

Harrison placed his big hands on the girl's tiny waist, letting her sense the weightlessness that would soon be hers.

And then, in an explosion of joy and grace, into the air they sprang!

Not only were the laws of the land abandoned, but the law of gravity and the laws of motion as well.

They reeled, whirled, swiveled, flounced, capered, gamboled, and spun.

They leaped like deer on the moon.

The studio ceiling was thirty feet high, but each leap brought the dancers nearer to it. It became their obvious intention to kiss the ceiling.

They kissed it.

And then, neutralizing gravity with love and pure will, they remained suspended in air inches below the ceiling, and they kissed each other for a long, long time.

6 It was then that Diana Moon Glampers, the Handicapper General, came into the studio with a double-barreled ten-gauge shotgun. She fired twice, and the Emperor and the Empress were dead before they hit the floor.

Diana Moon Glampers loaded the gun again. She aimed it at the musicians and told them they had ten seconds to get their handicaps back on.

It was then that the Bergerons' television tube burned out.

Hazel turned to comment about the blackout to George.

But George had gone out into the kitchen for a can of beer.

George came back in with the beer, paused while a handicap signal shook him up. And then he sat down again. "You been crying?" he said to Hazel.

"Yup." she said,

"What about?" he said.

"I forget." she said. "Something real sad on television."

"What was it?" he said.

"It's all kind of mixed up in my mind." said Hazel.

"Forget sad things." said George.

"I always do." said Hazel.

"That's my girl." said George. He winced. There was the sound of a riveting gun in his head.

"Gee ___ I could tell that one was a doozy." said Hazel.

"You can say that again." said George.

"Gee ___ " said Hazel, "I could tell that one was a doozy."

Comprehension Check-Up Questions

1. What is the job of U.S. H-G and her agents? (section 1)

2. How equal are people in 2081?

3. How smart are George, Harrison, and Hazel?

4. Why can't George and Hazel remember their son's arrest?

5. Even if she sheds tears, Hazel does not know why she is crying. Why not? (section 2)

6. Why does George's mental handicapper ring a noise when he watches ballerinas?

7. Does Hazel wear a handicapper? Why or why not?

8. How different noises are made in George's mental handicapper? Why are they set different?

9. What handicapper does George wear around his neck? What is the function of that apparatus? (section 3)

10. Why does George refuse to take away his handicapper for a moment with Hazel's connivance?

11. Why does the announcer hand the bulletin to a ballerina? (section 4)

12. Why does the ballerina apologize for her beautiful voice?

A Hanging

George Orwell

Eric Arthur Blair (1903–1950), better known by his pen name **George Orwell**, was an English novelist and essayist, journalist and critic, whose work is characterised by lucid prose, awareness of social injustice, opposition to totalitarianism, and outspoken support of democratic socialism. As a writer, Orwell produced literary criticism and poetry, fiction and polemical journalism; and is best known for the allegorical novella *Animal Farm* (1945) and the dystopian novel *Nineteen Eighty-Four* (1949). His non-fiction works, including *The Road to Wigan Pier* (1937), documenting his experience of working-class life in the north of England, and *Homage to Catalonia* (1938), an account of his experiences soldiering for the Republican faction of the Spanish Civil War (1936–1939), are as critically respected as his essays on politics and literature, language and culture. In 2008, *The Times* ranked George Orwell second among "The 50 greatest British writers since 1945". Orwell's work remains influential in popular culture and in political culture, and the adjective "Orwellian" — describing totalitarian and authoritarian social practices — is part of the English language, like many of his neologisms, such as "Big Brother", "Thought Police" and "Hate week", "Room 101", the "memory hole" and "Newspeak ", "doublethink" and "proles", "unperson" and "thoughtcrime".

"A Hanging" (1931) was first published in August 1931 in the British literary magazine *The Adelphi*. Set in Burma, where Orwell had served in the British Imperial Police from 1922 to 1927, it describes the execution of a criminal. The condemned man is given no name, nor is it explained what crime he has committed. For the British police who supervise his execution, the hanging is an unpleasant but routine piece of business. The narrator takes no active part in the hanging, and appears to be less experienced than his colleagues. As the prisoner is marched and handcuffed to the gallows he steps slightly aside to avoid treading in a puddle of rainwater; the narrator sees this, and deeply touched. However, the sentence is carried out, and all concerned feel a sudden relief as they leave the scene where the dead man still hangs. (*adapted from Wikipedia*)

Vocabulary

sodden	gallow
condemned	warders
except for	magistrates and the like
a puny wisp	come goodness knows whence
fixed bayonets	a young Eurasian jailer
a careful, caressing grip	the mystery . . . of cutting a life short
yielding his arms limply	in full tide
a bugle call	convicts
head jailor	most disagreeable

1   It was in Burma, a sodden morning of the rains. A sickly light, like yellow tinfoil, was slanting over the high walls into the jail yard. We were waiting outside the condemned cells, a row of sheds fronted with double bars, like small animal cages. Each cell measured about ten feet by ten and was quite bare except for a plank bed and a pot of drinking water. In some of them brown silent men were squatting at the inner bars, with their blankets draped round them. These were the condemned men, due to be hanged within the next week or two.

2   One prisoner had been brought out of his cell. He was a Hindu, a puny wisp of a man, with a shaven head and vague liquid eyes. He had a thick, sprouting moustache, absurdly too big for his body, rather like the moustache of a comic man on the films. Six tall Indian warders were guarding him and getting him ready for the gallows. Two of them stood by with rifles and fixed bayonets, while the others handcuffed him, passed a chain through his handcuffs and fixed it to their belts, and lashed his arms tight to his sides. They crowded very close about him, with their hands always on him in a careful, caressing grip, as though all the while feeling him to make sure he was there. It was like men handling a fish which is still alive and may jump back into the water. But he stood quite unresisting, yielding his arms limply to the ropes, as though he hardly noticed what was happening.

3   Eight o'clock struck and a bugle call, desolately thin in the wet air, floated from the distant barracks. The superintendent of the jail, who was standing apart from the rest of us, moodily prodding the gravel with his stick, raised his head at the sound. He was an army doctor, with a grey toothbrush moustache and a gruff voice. 'For God's sake hurry up, Francis." he said irritably. 'The man ought to have been dead by this time. Aren't you ready yet?'

4   Francis, the head jailer, a fat Dravidian in a white drill suit and gold spectacles,[1] waved his black hand. 'Yes sir, yes sir.', he bubbled. 'All iss satisfactorily prepared. The hangman iss waiting. We shall proceed.'

'Well, quick march, then. The prisoners can't get their breakfast till this job's over.'

5   We set out for the gallows. Two warders marched on either side of the prisoner, with their rifles at the slope[2]; two others marched close against him, gripping him by arm and shoulder, as though at once pushing and supporting him.[3] The rest of us, magistrates and the like, followed behind. Suddenly,

---

1) 흰 목면 제복과 금테 안경을 쓴 드라비디안. Dravidian [drəvidiən] n.드라비다 사람(인도 남부나 Ceylon섬에 사는 비(非)아리안계 종족)
2) 총을 비스듬히 차고.
3) 사형수를 밀면서 동시에 부축하는 듯이.

when we had gone ten yards, the procession stopped short without any order or warning. A dreadful thing had happened ___ a dog, come goodness knows whence, had appeared in the yard. It came bounding among us with a loud volley of barks,[4] and leapt round us wagging its whole body, wild with glee at finding so many human beings together. It was a large woolly dog, half Airedale, half pariah. For a moment it pranced round us, and then, before anyone could stop it, it had made a dash for the prisoner, and jumping up tried to lick his face. Everyone stood aghast, too taken aback even to grab at the dog.[5]

'Who let that bloody brute in here?' said the superintendent angrily. 'Catch it, someone!'

6   A warder, detached from the escort, charged clumsily after the dog, but it danced and gambolled just out of his reach, taking everything as part of the game. A young Eurasian jailer picked up a handful of gravel and tried to stone the dog away, but it dodged the stones and came after us again. Its yaps echoed from the jail wails. The prisoner, in the grasp of the two warders, looked on incuriously, as though this was another formality of the hanging. It was several minutes before someone managed to catch the dog. Then we put my handkerchief

---

4) rf. a volley of questions. 빗발치는 질문들.
5) 넋이 나가 개를 잡지도 못하다. rf. He was much taken with her beauty.

through its collar and moved off once more, with the dog still straining and whimpering.

7   It was about forty yards to the gallows. I watched the bare brown back of the prisoner marching in front of me. He walked clumsily with his bound arms, but quite steadily, with that bobbing gait of the Indian who never straightens his knees. At each step his muscles slid neatly into place, the lock of hair on his scalp danced up and down, his feet printed themselves on the wet gravel. And once, in spite of the men who gripped him by each shoulder, he stepped slightly aside to avoid a puddle on the path.

8 It is curious, but till that moment I had never realized what it means to destroy a healthy, conscious man. When I saw the prisoner step aside to avoid the puddle, I saw the mystery, the unspeakable wrongness, of cutting a life short when it is in full tide. This man was not dying, he was alive just as we were alive. All the organs of his body were working ___ bowels digesting food, skin renewing itself, nails growing, tissues forming ___ all toiling away in solemn foolery. His nails would still be growing when he stood on the drop, when he was falling through the air with a tenth of a second to live. His eyes saw the yellow gravel and the grey walls, and his brain still

remembered, foresaw, reasoned ___ reasoned even about puddles. He and we were a party of men walking together, seeing, hearing, feeling, understanding the same world; and in two minutes, with a sudden snap, one of us would be gone ___ one mind less, one world less.[6]

9   The gallows stood in a small yard, separate from the main grounds of the prison, and overgrown with tall prickly weeds. It was a brick erection like three sides of a shed[7], with planking on top, and above that two beams and a crossbar with the rope[8] dangling. The hangman, a grey-haired convict in the white uniform of the prison, was waiting beside his machine. He greeted us with a servile crouch[9] as we entered. At a word from Francis the two warders, gripping the prisoner more closely than ever, half led, half pushed him to the gallows and helped him clumsily up the ladder. Then the hangman climbed up and fixed the rope round the prisoner's neck.

10   We stood waiting, five yards away. The warders had formed in a rough circle round the gallows. And then, when the noose was fixed, the prisoner began crying out on his god.

---

6) (죄수의 죽음과 더불어) 하나의 생명이 사라지고 또한 한 세계도 사라진다.
7) 마치 벽이 세 개로 된 헛간 같이 생긴 벽돌 구조물(erection).
8) 그 제일 윗면에 널빤지가 있고 널빤지 위로 기둥 두 개와 밧줄이 달린 (기둥 사이에 연결된) 가로대.
9) 공손히 허리를 조아리며. rf. He crouched to his master.

It was a high, reiterated cry of 'Ram! Ram! Ram! Ram!', not urgent and fearful like a prayer or a cry for help, but steady, rhythmical, almost like the tolling of a bell. The dog answered the sound with a whine. The hangman, still standing on the gallows, produced a small cotton bag like a flour bag and drew it down over the prisoner's face. But the sound, muffled by the cloth, still persisted, over and over again: 'Ram! Ram! Ram! Ram! Ram!'

11 The hangman climbed down and stood ready, holding the lever. Minutes seemed to pass. The steady, muffled crying from the prisoner went on and on, 'Ram! Ram! Ram!' never faltering for an instant. The superintendent, his head on his chest, was slowly poking the ground with his stick; perhaps he was counting the cries, allowing the prisoner a fixed number ___ fifty, perhaps, or a hundred. Everyone had changed colour. The Indians had gone grey like bad coffee, and one or two of the bayonets were wavering. We looked at the lashed, hooded man on the drop, and listened to his cries ___ each cry another second of life; the same thought was in all our minds: oh, kill him quickly, get it over, stop that abominable noise!

12 Suddenly the superintendent made up his mind. Throwing up his head he made a swift motion with his stick. 'Chalo!' he

shouted almost fiercely.

There was a clanking noise, and then dead silence. The prisoner had vanished, and the rope was twisting on itself. I let go of the dog, and it galloped immediately to the back of the gallows; but when it got there it stopped short, barked, and then retreated into a corner of the yard, where it stood among the weeds, looking timorously out at us. We went round the gallows to inspect the prisoner's body. He was dangling with his toes pointed straight downwards, very slowly revolving, as dead as a stone.

13 The superintendent reached out with his stick and poked the bare body; it oscillated, slightly. 'He's all right.', said the superintendent. He backed out from under the gallows, and blew out a deep breath. The moody look had gone out of his face quite suddenly. He glanced at his wrist-watch. 'Eight minutes past eight. Well, that's all for this morning, thank God.'

14 The warders unfixed bayonets and marched away. The dog, sobered and conscious of having misbehaved itself, slipped after them. We walked out of the gallows yard, past the condemned cells with their waiting prisoners, into the big central yard of the prison. The convicts, under the command of warders armed with lathis, were already receiving their

breakfast. They squatted in long rows, each man holding a tin pannikin, while two warders with buckets marched round ladling out rice; it seemed quite a homely, jolly scene, after the hanging. An enormous relief had come upon us now that the job was done. One felt an impulse to sing, to break into a run, to snigger. All at once everyone began chattering gaily.

15 The Eurasian walking beside me nodded towards the way we had come, with a knowing smile: 'Do you know, sir, our friend (he meant the dead man), when he heard his appeal had been dismissed, he pissed on the floor of his cell. From fright. Kindly take one of my cigarettes, sir. Do you not admire my new silver case, sir? From the boxwallah, two rupees eight annas. Classy European style.'

Several people laughed ____ at what, nobody seemed certain.

Francis was walking by the superintendent, talking garrulously. 'Well, sir, all hass passed off with the utmost satisfactoriness. It wass all finished ____ flick! like that. It iss not always so ____ oah, no! I have known cases where the doctor wass obliged to go beneath the gallows and pull the prisoner's legs to ensure decease. Most disagreeable!'

'Wriggling about, eh? That's bad.', said the superintendent.

'Ach, sir, it iss worse when they become refractory! One man, I recall, clung to the bars of hiss cage when we went to take him out. You will scarcely credit, sir, that it took six warders to dislodge him, three pulling at each leg. We reasoned with him. "My dear fellow." we said, "think of all the pain and trouble you are causing to us!" But no, he would not listen! Ach, he wass very troublesome!'

I found that I was laughing quite loudly. Everyone was laughing. Even the superintendent grinned in a tolerant way. 'You'd better all come out and have a drink.', he said quite genially. 'I've got a bottle of whisky in the car. We could do with it.'

We went through the big double gates of the prison, into the road. 'Pulling at his legs!' exclaimed a Burmese magistrate suddenly, and burst into a loud chuckling. We all began laughing again. At that moment Francis's anecdote seemed extraordinarily funny. We all had a drink together, native and European alike, quite amicably. The dead man was a hundred yards away.

Comprehension Check-Up Questions

1. When and where does the story take place? (section 1)

2. Who are they in the prison?

3. How does the prisoner look like? (section 2)

4. How many warders guard the man and how do they treat him?

5. Of what nationalities are the warders?

6. What does the superintendent do? (section 3)

7. How does he look like and how does he seem to feel about this job?

8. Of what nationality do you guess he is?

9. Who is Francis? How does he look? How is his English? (section 4)

10. What do you think his language and attitude tell about him?

11. What happens and how do the people respond to it? (section 5)

12. What does the prisoner do at his execution? (section 11)

13. How do the people behave confronted with the prisoner's chanting? (section 12)

14. How do people feel about being back to a normal life? (section 14)

Senor Payroll

William E. Barrettt

"Senor payroll" is a story of a certain company which has employed a group of expert stokers who are Mexicans. The stokers continually ask for salary advances and when an order to only give advances to genuine emergency cases is released, the stokers fake so many emergencies claiming sick wives, children and aunts. This forces the company to give another order that limits the salary advances to those who wish to resign from the company. A series of resignations and reassignments follows as the stokers quit and apply for new jobs in the same company. Another order is released that says that no stoker will be reassigned after quitting until 30 days are over. The stokers continue to quit coming back to be rehired using fictitious names. The company is left with no choice and stops to gives any other orders. The story is narrated by one of the company's clerks who, together with his colleague Larry are forced to have workloads of paperwork due to numerous requests for salary advances by the shrewd Mexican stokers who can barely wait for pay day. They work very hard and offer excellent services but have continually disturbed their employers with the requests. In an effort to curb this nuisance behavior, the company gives numerous orders that all fail to rectify the situation.

(adapted from https://writeanessay-forme.com/senor-payroll-by-william-e-barrette/)

Vocabulary

bewildering array	retorts
paymaster	shovels
stokers	pressure nozzel
Herculean	stripped to the waist
shifts	miser
veins	handy gangs
advance	foreman
pay check	wringing
memorandum	the Almighty
veritable	shovel
epidemic	dissuade
gravely	without a flicker
transient workers	duel

1 Larry and I were Junior Engineers in the gas plant, which means that we were clerks. Anything that could be classified as paper work came to the flat double desk across which we faced each other. The main office downtown sent us a bewildering array of orders and rules that were to be put into effect.

Junior Engineers were beneath the notice of everyone except the Mexican laborers at the plant. To them we were the visible form of a distant, unknowable paymaster. We were Senor Payroll.

Those Mexicans were great workmen: the aristocrats among them were the stokers, big men who worked Herculean eight-hours shifts in the fierce heat of the retorts. They scooped coal with huge shovels and hurled it with uncanny aim at tiny doors. The coal streamed out from the shovels like black water from a high pressure nozzle, and never missed the narrow opening. The stokers worked stripped to the waist, and there was pride and dignity in them. Few men could do such work, and they were the few.

The Company paid its men only twice a month, on the fifth and on the twentieth. To a Mexican, this was absurd. What man with money will make it last 15 days? If he hoarded money beyond the spending of three days, he was a miser-and when, Senor, did the blood of Spain flow in the veins of misers? Hence it was the custom for our stokers to appear every third or fourth day to draw the money due to them.

2 There was a certain elasticity in the Company rules, and Larry and I sent the necessary forms to the Main Office and received an "advance" against a man's pay check. Then, one day, Downtown favored us with a memorandum:

"There have been too many abuses of the advance-against-wages privilege. Hereafter, no advance against wages will be made to any employee except in a case of genuine emergency."

We had no sooner posted the notice when in came stoker Juan Garcia. He asked for an advance. I pointed to the notice. He spelled it through slowly, then said, "what does this mean, this genuine emergency?"

I explained to him patiently that the Company was kind and sympathetic, but that it was a great nuisance to have to pay wages every few days. If someone was ill or if money was urgently needed for some other good reason, then the Company would make an exception to the rule.

Juan Garcia turned his hat over and over slowly in his big hands. "I do not get my money?"

"Next payday, Juan. On the 20th."

He went out silently and I felt a little ashamed of myself. I looked across the desk at Larry. He avoided my eyes.

In the next hour two other stokers came in, looked at the notice, had it explained and walked solemnly out; then no more came. What we did not know was that Juan Garcia, Pete Mendoza and Francisco Gonzalez had spread the word and that every Mexican in the plant was explaining the order to every other Mexican. "To get the money now, the wife must be sick. There must be medicine for the baby."

The next morning Juan Garcia's wife was practically dying, Pete Mendonza's mother would hardly last the day, there was a veritable epidemic among children and, just for variety,[1] there was one sick father. We always suspected that the old man was really sick; no Mexican would otherwise have thought of him.[2] At any rate, nobody paid Larry and me to examine private lives; we made out our forms with an added line describing the "genuine emergency". Our people got paid.

That went on for a week. Then came a new order, curt and to the point: "Hereafter, employees will be paid only on the 5th and the 20th of the month. No exceptions will be made except in the cases of employees leaving the service of the Company."

The notice went up on the board and we explained its significance gravely. "No Juan Garcia, we cannot advance your wages. It is too bad about your wife and your cousins and your aunts, but there is a new rule."

Juan Garcia went out and thought it over. He thought out loud with Mendoza and Gonzalez and Ayala, then, in the morning, he was back. "I am quitting this company for different job. You pay me now?"

We argued that it was a good company and that it loved its

---

1) 구색용으로.
2) 그 아버지(old man)가 아프다고 우리도 그렇게 추측해 왔고 다른 멕시칸들도 그렇게 생각했을 것이다.

employees like children, but in the end we paid off, because Juan Garcia quit. And so did Gonzalez, Mendoza Obregon, Ayala and Ortez, the best stokers, men who could not be replaced.

Larry and I looked at each other; we knew what was coming in about three days. One of our duties was to sit on the hiring line early each morning, engaging transient workers for the handy gangs. Never before had we been called upon to hire such skilled virtuosos as stokers for handy gang work, but we were called upon to hire them now.

The day foreman was wringing his hands and asking the Almighty if he was personally supposed to shovel this condemned coal, while there in a stolid, patient line were skilled men — "Garcia, Mendoza and others" waiting to be hired. We hired them, of course. There was nothing else to do.

Every day we had a line of resigning stokers, and another line of stokers seeking work. Our paper work became very complicated. At the Main Office they were jumping up and down. The procession of forms showing Juan Garcia's resigning and being hired over and over again was too much for them. Sometimes Downtown had Garcia on the payroll twice at the same time when someone down there was slow in entering a resignation. Our phone rang early and often.

Tolerantly and patiently we explaining: "There's nothing we can do if a man wants to quit, and if there are stokers available when the plant needs stokers, we hire them."

3 Out of chaos, Downtown issued another order. I read it and whistled. Larry looked at it and said, "It is going to be very quiet around here."

The order read: "Hereafter, no employee who resigns may be rehired within a period of 30 days."

Juan Garcia was due for another resignation, and when he came in we showed him the order and explained that standing in line the next day would do him no good if he resigned today. "Thirty days is a long time, Juan."

It was a grave matter and he took time to reflect on it. So did Gonzalez, Mendoza, Ayala and Ortez. Ultimately, however, they were all back-and all resigned.

We did our best to dissuade them and we were sad about the parting. This time it was for keeps and they shook hands with us solemnly. It was very nice knowing us. Larry and I looked at each other when they were gone and we both knew that neither of us had been pulling for Downtown to win this duel. It was a blue day.

In the morning, however, they were all back in line. With the utmost gravity, Juan Garcia informed me that he was a stoker looking for a job.

"No dice, Juan." I said. "Come back in 30 days. I warned you."

His eyes looked straight into mine without a flicker. "There is some mistake, Senor." he said. "I am Manual Hernandez. I work as the stoker in Pueblo, in Santa Fe, in many places."

I stared back at him, remembering the sick wife and the babies without medicine, the mother-in-law in the hospital, the many resignations and the rehiring. I knew that there was a gas plant in Pueblo, and that there was not any in Santa Fe; but who was I to argue with a man about his own name? A stoker is a stoker.

So I hired him. I hired Gonzalez, too, who swore that his name was Carrera, and Ayala, who had shamelessly become Smith.

Three days later, the resigning started.

Within a week our payroll read like a history of Latin America. Everyone was on it: Lopez and Obregon, Villa, Diaz, Batista, Gomez, and even San Martin and Bolivar. Finally Larry and I, growing weary of starting at familiar faces and writing unfamiliar names, went to the Superintendent and told the whole story. He tried not to grin, and said, "Damned nonsense!"

4 The next day the orders were taken down. We called our most prominent stokers into the office and pointed to the board. No rules any more.

"The next time we hire you hombres." Larry said grimly, "come in under the names you like best, because, that's the way you are going to stay on the books."

They looked at us and they looked at the board: then for the first time in the long duel, their teeth flashed write. "Si, Senores." They said. And so it was.

Comprehension Check-Up Questions

1. What company does the narrator work for? What kind of work do the narrator says that he and Larry actually do as "Junior Engineers"? (section 1)

2. What kind of work do the Mexican laborers do and how well do they do it?

3. What is the original paydays policy of company and what is the problem of Mexican laborers about it?

4. Why does the company decide to reject the workers' request of advance? How is the new policy known to everybody? (section 2)

5. How does the narrator feel about the whole situation?

6. What strategy do the Mexicans employ to get advances and how do the narrator and his coworker respond to it?

7. What is the second company order in terms of payment? (section 3)

8. How are the Mexicans dealing with it and what difficulty does it bring to the narrator and Larry?

9. What is the third order of the company?

10. How do the workers respond to the third order? How does the narrator feel about it?

11. How does the company's 30-day rule end?

The Storm

Kate Chopin

Kate Chopin (/ˈʃoʊpæn/;1850–1904) was an American author of short stories and novels based in Louisiana. She is now considered by some scholars to have been a forerunner of American 20th-century feminist authors.

Of maternal French and paternal Irish descent, Chopin was born in St. Louis, Missouri. She married and moved with her husband to New Orleans. They later lived in the country in Cloutierville, Louisiana. From 1892 to 1895, Chopin wrote short stories for both children and adults that were published in several noted magazines. Her stories aroused controversy because of her subjects and her approach; they were condemned as immoral by some critics. Her major works were two short story collections: *Bayou Folk* (1894) and *A Night in Acadie* (1897). Her important short stories included "Désirée's Baby" (1893), a tale of miscegenation in antebellum Louisiana, "The Story of an Hour" (1894), and "The Storm" (1898). Chopin also wrote two novels: *At Fault* (1890) and *The Awakening* (1899). Within a decade of her death, Chopin was widely recognized as one of the leading writers of her time.

"The Storm" is a short story written in 1898. The story takes place during the 19th century in the South of the United States, where storms are frequent and dangerous. It did not appear in print in Chopin's lifetime, but it was published in *The Complete Works of Kate Chopin* in 1969. "The Storm" is a story of sexual desire, a topic not publicly discussed in the 19th century, written in a third-person omniscient point of view. The relationship between Calixta and Alcée holds a degree of passion that is absent from both of their marriages. Calixta is scared of the storm, but Alcée's calmness relaxes her. When Alcée embraces her after the lightning hits a chinaberry tree, it reminds her of the love she once had for Alcée: "A bolt struck a tall chinaberry tree at the edge of the field. It filled all visible space with a blinding glare and the crash seemed to invade the very boards they stood upon." Calixta's sexual desire is directly tied to the storm (*adapted from Wikipedia*).

Vocabulary

piped	nigh
occupied	resort to
gallery	immaculate dove
rode in	the roar of the elements
side projection	revelation
startled	yield
vivacity	cistern
white, monumental bed	brogans
pomegranate seed	

I

The leaves were so still that even Bibi thought it was going to rain. Bobinot, who was accustomed to converse on terms of perfect equality with his little son, called the child's attention to certain sombre clouds that were rolling with sinister intention from the west, accompanied by a sullen, threatening roar. They were at Friedheimer's store and decided to remain there till the storm had passed. They sat within the door on two empty kegs. Bibi was four years old and looked very wise.

"Mama'll be afraid, yes." he said with blinking eyes.[1]

"She'll shut the house. Maybe she got Sylvie[2] helping her this evening." Bobinot responded reassuringly.

"No; she hasn't got Sylvie. Sylvie was helping her yesterday." piped Bibi.[3]

Bobinot arose and going across to the counter purchased a can of shrimps, of which Calixta was very fond. Then he returned to the keg and sat calmly holding the can of shrimps while the storm burst. It shook the wooden store and seemed to be ripping great furrows in the distant field.[4] Bibi laid his little hand on his father's knee and was not afraid.

---

1) 눈을 깜빡이며.
2) 하녀 이름.
3) piped 조잘거렸다.
4) 저 먼 들판에 거대한 이랑을 파듯.

II

Calixta, at home, felt no uneasiness[5] for their safety. She sat at a side window sewing on a sewing machine. She was greatly occupied and did not notice the approaching storm. But she felt very warm and often stopped to mop her face on which the perspiration gathered in beads.[6] It began to grow dark, and suddenly realizing the situations,[7] she got up hurriedly and went about closing windows and doors.

Out on the small front gallery she had hung Bobinot's Sunday clothes to dry and she hastened out to gather them before the rain fell. As she stepped outside, Alcee Laballiere rode in at the gate. She had not seen him very often since her marriage, and never alone. She stood there with Bobinot's coat in her hands, and the big rain drops began to fall. Alcee rode his horse under the shelter of a side projection where the chickens had huddled and there were plows and a harrow piled up in the corner.

"May I come and wait on your gallery till the storm is over, Calixta?" he asked.

Come 'long in, M'sieur Alcee."

His voice and her own startled her as if from a trance, and

---

5) 걱정하지 않았다는 뜻.
6) 땀이 구슬처럼 맺혀있는 얼굴.
7) storm이 온다는 사실.

she seized Bobinot's vest. Alcee, mounting to the porch,[8] grabbed the trousers and snatched Bibi's jacket that was about to be carried away by a sudden gust of wind. He expressed an intention to remain outside, but it was soon apparent that he might as well have been out in the open:[9] the water beat in upon the boards in driving sheets,[10] and he went inside, closing the door after him. It was even necessary to put something beneath the door to keep the water out.

"My! what a rain! It's good two years since it rain' like that." exclaimed Calixta.

She was a little fuller of figure[11] than five years before when she married; but she had lost nothing of her vivacity. Her blue eyes still retained their melting quality; and her yellow hair, dishevelled by the wind and rain,[12] kinked more stubbornly than ever about her ears and temples.

The rain beat upon the low, shingled roof with a force and clatter.[13] It threatened to break an entrance and deluge them there. They were in the dining room. Adjoining was her bed room,[14] with Bibi's couch alongside her own. The door stood

---

8) 현관으로 올라서면서.

9) 밖에 있다 가겠다고 의사표시 하였지만 곧 그것(집 밖/주랑에 잠시 서 있는 것)은 노천에 있는 것이나 마찬가지라는 것이 분명해졌다.

10) 펼쳐놓은 천이 날아 들어오듯이/엄청 많이/바닥으로 빗줄기가 들이쳐 왔다.

11) 몸이 더 풍만해졌다.

12) 비바람에 마구 흐트러진 채.

13) 비는 힘과 요란한 소리로 낮게 이엉을 이언 지붕 위로 내려쳤다.

open, and the room with its white, monumental bed looked dim and mysterious.

Alcee flung himself into a rocker and Calixta nervously began to gather up[15] from the floor the cotton sheet which she had been sewing.

"If this keeps up, Dieu sait[16] if the leaves are goining to stand it!" she exclaimed.

"What have you got to do with the leaves?"

"I got enough to do! And there's Bobinot with Bibi out in that storm. If he only didn't left Friedheimer's!"

"Let us hope, Calixta, that Bobinot's got sense enough to come in out of a cyclone."

She went and stood at the window with a greatly disturbed look on her face. She wiped the frame that was clouded with moisture. It was stiflingly hot. Alcee got up and joined her at the window, looking over her shoulder. The rain was coming down in sheets obscuring the view of far-off cabins and enveloping the distant wood in a gray mist. The playing of the lightning was incessant. A bolt struck a tall chinaberry tree at the edge of the field. It filled all visible space with a blinding glare[17] and the crash seemed to invade the very boards they stood upon.

---

14) (다이닝룸 옆으로) 침실이 붙어있었다.
15) gather up의 목적어는 the cotton sheet 이하.
16) God knows.
17) 눈이 멀 것 같은 강렬한 광채.

Calixta put her hands to her eyes, and with a cry, staggered backward. Alcee's arm encircled her, and for an instant he drew her close to him.

"Bonte!" she cried, releasing herself from his encircling arm and retreating from the window, "the house'll go next! If I only knew where Bibi was!" She would not compose herself; she would not be seated. Alcee clasped her shoulders and looked into her face. The contact of her warm body had aroused all the old-time infatuation and desire for her flesh.

"Calixta." he said, "don't be frightened. Nothing can happen. The house is too low to be struck, with so many tall trees standing about. There! aren't you going to be quiet? say, aren't you?" He pushed her hair back from her face that was warm and steaming. Her lips were as red and moist as pomegranate seed. Her white neck and a glimpse of her full, firm bosom disturbed him powerfully. As she glanced up at him the fear in her liquid blue eyes had given place to a drowsy gleam that unconsciously betrayed a sensuous desire. He looked down into her eyes and there was nothing for him to do but to gather her lips in a kiss. It reminded him of Assumption.

"Do you remember ___ in Assumption,[18) Calixta?" he asked in a low voice broken by passion. Oh! she remembered; for in Assumption he had kissed her and kissed and kissed her; until

---

18) 지역 이름.

his senses would well nigh fail, and to save her he would resort to a desperate flight. If she was not an immaculate dove in those days, she was still inviolate; a passionate creature whose very defenselessness had made her defense, against which his honor forbade him to prevail. Now ___ well, now ___ her lips seemed in a manner free to be tasted, as well as her round, white throat and her whiter breasts.

They did not heed the crashing torrents, and the roar of the elements made her laugh as she lay in his arms. She was a revelation in that dim, mysterious chamber; as white as the couch she lay upon. Her firm, elastic flesh that was knowing[19] for the first time its birthright, was like a creamy lily that the sun invites to contribute its breath and perfume to the undying life of the world.[20]

The generous abundance of her passion, without guile or trickery, was like a white flame which penetrated and found response in depths of his own sensuous nature that had never yet been reached.

When he touched her breasts they gave themselves up in quivering ecstasy, inviting his lips. Her mouth was a fountain of delight. And when he possessed her, they seemed to swoon together at the very borderland of life's mystery.

---

19) know의 목적어는 its birthright.
20) 태양이 세상의 생명에 그(lily) 숨결과 향을 주라고 초대한 크림색 백합 같았다.

He stayed cushioned upon her, breathless, dazed, enervated, with his heart beating like a hammer upon her. With one hand she clasped his head, her lips lightly touching his forehead. The other hand stroked with a soothing rhythm his muscular shoulders.

The growl of the thunder was distant and passing away. The rain beat softly upon the shingles, inviting them to drowsiness and sleep. But they dared not yield.[21]

The rain was over; and the sun was turning the glistening green world into a palace of gems. Calixta, on the gallery, watched Alcee ride away. He turned and smiled at her with a beaming face; and she lifted her pretty chin in the air and laughed aloud.

III

Bobinot and Bibi, trudging home, stopped at the cistern to make themselves clean.

"My! Bibi, what will your mama say? You ought to be ashamed. You should not have put on those good pants. Look at them! And that mud on your collar! How you got that mud on your collar, Bibi? I never saw such a boy!" Bobinot was the

---

21) drowsiness와 sleep에 굴복하다/즉 잠들어버릴 수가 없었다.

embodiment of serious solicitude[22] as he strove to remove mud from his own person and his son's ___ the signs of their tramp over heavy roads and through wet fields. He scraped the mud off Bibi's bare legs and feet with a stick and carefully removed all traces from his heavy brogans. Then, prepared for the scold of Calixa, they entered cautiously at the back door.

Calixta was preparing supper. She had set the table and was dripping coffee at the hearth. She sprang up as they came in.

"Oh, Bobinot! You back! My! I was worried. Where have you been during the rain? And Bibi? he isn't wet? he isn't hurt?" She had clasped Bibi and was kissing him again and again. Bobinot's explanations and apologies which he had been composing all along the way, died on his lips as Calixta felt him to see if he were dry and all right.

"I brought you some shrimps, Calixta." offered Bobinot, hauling the can from his ample side pocket and laying it on the table.

"Shrimps! Oh, Bobinot! you are so nice!" and she gave him a smacking kiss on the cheek, "We'll have a party to-night! umph-umph!"

Bobinot and Bibi began to relax and enjoy themselves, and when the three seated themselves at table they laughed much and so loud that anyone might have heard them far away.

---

22) 진지한 간청의 화신/매우 친절하게 아이를 다룸.

IV

Alcee Laballiere wrote to his wife, Clarisse, that night. It was a loving letter, full of tender solicitude. He told her not to hurry back, but if she and the babies liked it at Biloxi, to stay a month longer. He was getting on nicely; and though he missed them, he was willing to bear the separation a while longer ___ because their health and pleasure were the first things to be considered.

V

As for Clarisse, she was charmed upon receiving her husband's letter. She and the babies were doing well. The society was agreeable; many of her old friends and acquaintances were there. And the first free breath since her marriage seemed to restore the pleasant liberty of her maiden days. Although she was devoted to her husband, their intimate conjugal life was something which she was willing to forego for a while.

Comprehension Check-Up Questions

1. Why did father and son decide to stay Friedheimer's store instead of going home? (part I)

2. How is the relationship of father and son?

3. What personalities do you guess they have?

4. What was Calixta doing while her husband and son were out? (part II)

5. Why did she go outside and find Alcee?

6. How come did Alcee go inside the house?

7. How does Calixta look? (refer to the paragraph beginning with "She was a little fuller . . .")

8. How do you describe their dialogue?

9. What led Calixta and Alcee to make physical contact?

10. What kind of relationship do you think they had before their marriages?

11. How did Bobinot and Bibi prepare themselves before they went inside the house? (part III)

12. How did Calixta meet them?

13. How much did the family enjoy the time?

A White Heron

Sarah Orne Jewett

Sarah Orne Jewett (1849–1909) was an American novelist, short story writer and poet, best known for her local color works set along or near the southern seacoast of Maine. Jewett is recognized as an important practitioner of American literary regionalism. Jewett's family had been residents of New England for many generations, and Sarah Orne Jewett was born in South Berwick, Maine. Jewett's father was a doctor and Jewett often accompanied him on his rounds, becoming acquainted with the sights and sounds of her native land and its people. In later life, Jewett often visited Boston, where she was acquainted with many of the most influential literary figures of her day; but she always returned to South Berwick.

At age 19, Jewett published her first important story in the *Atlantic Monthly*, and her reputation grew throughout the 1870s and 1880s. Her literary importance arises from her careful, if subdued, vignettes of country life that reflect a contemporary interest in local color rather than in plot. Jewett made her reputation with the novella *The Country of the Pointed Firs* (1896). *A Country Doctor* (1884), a novel reflecting her father and her early ambitions for a medical career, and *A White Heron* (1886), a collection of short stories are among her finest work. Jewett never married, but she established a close friendship with writer Annie Adams Fields (1834–1915) and her husband, publisher James Thomas Fields, editor of the *Atlantic Monthly*. After the sudden death of James Fields in 1881, Jewett and Annie Fields lived together for the rest of Jewett's life in what was then termed a "Boston marriage".

"A White Heron" is a short story by Sarah Orne Jewett. First published by Houghton, Mifflin and Company in 1886, it was soon collected as the title story in *A White Heron and Other Stories* follows a young city girl named Sylvia who came to live with her grandmother in the country. She meets a young ornithologist hunter seeking to find a rare bird that he recently spotted in the area. As the story progresses, Sylvia is challenged with whether or not she should tell the hunter she saw the bird. She also discovers her passion for country life and her love and values for the animals that inhabit it. "A White Heron" can be thought of as a starting point for both ecological, nature-ethical literature in the US, and questioning the undoubted positive development of the US. The author explores a number of ecological themes including the freedom of nature, a return to nature, emancipation from materialism and industrialism. The protagonist in "A White Heron" also can be seen as an example of a woman of power and embodying heroism. Some criticism has even acknowledged the fact that the main character of the story may have been loosely based on Jewett's life growing up. Losing her father encouraged a need to be a strong and powerful young girl. She created a character who expressed the female voice of the women of her time in a new perspective than traditionally published works (*adapted from Wikipedia*).

Vocabulary

hide and seek	fare better
whereabout	dwelling
mistress Moo	rebel at
browse	farmstead
manufacturing town	foresters
houseful of children	soft-footed
brook	woodchoppers
twilight moth	sturdy trees
horror-stricken	pine/oak/maple
gravity	harmless housebreaker
farmer-lads	main-mast
wayfare	pang
plain	

1 The woods were already filled with shadows one June evening, just before eight o'clock, though a bright sunset still glimmered faintly among the trunks of the trees. A little girl was driving home her cow, a plodding, dilatory, provoking creature but a valued companion for all that.[1] They were going away from the western light, and striking deep into the dark woods, but their feet were familiar with the path, and it was no matter whether their eyes could see it or not.

Through all summer days there was hardly a night when the old cow could be found waiting at the pasture; on the contrary, it was her greatest pleasure to hide herself away among the high huckleberry bushes. Though she wore a loud bell she stood perfectly still so that the bell did not ring. So Sylvia had to hunt for her until she found her, and call Co'! Co'! The cow did not answer "Moo" until Silvia's childish patience was quite spent. It was a sort of hide and seek for them. Siliva enjoyed it a lot, for she had no playmates around. Sometimes this hide and seek had been so long that the cow herself had given an unusual signal of her whereabouts. Then Sylvia had only laughed to find Mistress Moo and urged her affectionately

---

1) a plodding, dilatory, provoking creature but a valued companion for all that
천천히 굼뜨게 걸으면서 짜증나게 하는 동물/소이지만 그럼에도 불구하고 귀한 친구.

homeward with a twig of birch leaves. The old cow was not inclined to wander farther,[2] she even turned in the right direction once as they left the pasture, and stepped along the road at a good pace. She was quite ready to be milked now, and seldom stopped to browse.

Sylvia wondered what her grandmother would say because they were so late. It was a great while since she had left home at half past five o'clock, but everybody knew the difficulty of making this errand a short one.[3] Mrs. Tilley was only thankful as she waited, for she had Sylvia, nowadays, to give such valuable assistance. It was a fun for Sylvia to live in the country after eight years in a crowded manufacturing town. For Sylvia herself, it seemed as if she never had been alive at all in the city before she came to live at the farm. She thought often of a wretched dry geranium that belonged to a town neighbor.

2 "'Afraid of folks.'" old Mrs. Tilley said to herself, with a smile, after she had chosen Sylvia from her daughter's houseful of children and was returning to the farm. "'Afraid of folks,' they said! I guess she won't be troubled with them in the country!" When they reached the door of the lonely house and

---

2) not inclined to wander farther 더 이상 도망 다닐 생각을 않고.
3) everybody knew the difficulty of making this errand a short one 이 일[소를 찾아 집으로 데려오는 일]이 빨리 되는 일이 아니라는 것을 알 사람은 다 안다.

stopped to unlock it, and the cat came to purr loudly, and rub against them, a deserted pussy, indeed, but fat with young robins, Sylvia whispered that this was a beautiful place to live in, and she never should wish to go home.

3　Sylvia and the cow followed the shady woodroad, the cow taking slow steps, and the girl very fast ones. The cow stopped long at the brook to drink, and Sylvia stood still and waited, letting her bare feet cool themselves in the shallow water, while the great twilight moths struck softly against her. She walked on through the brook as the cow moved away, and listened to the thrushes with a heart that beat fast with pleasure. There was a stirring in the great boughs overhead. They were full of little birds that seemed to be wide-awake, or else saying good-night to each other in sleepy twitters. Sylvia herself felt sleepy as she walked along. However, it was not much farther to the house, and the air was soft and sweet. She was not often in the woods so late as this, and it made her feel as if she were a part of the gray shadows and the moving leaves. She was just thinking how long it seemed since she first came to the farm a year ago, and wondering if everything went on in the noisy town just the same as when she was there; the thought of the great red-faced boy who used to chase and frighten her made her hurry along the path to escape from the shadow of the trees.

4 Suddenly Sylvia is horror-stricken to hear a clear whistle not very far away. Not a bird's whistle, which would have a sort of friendliness, but a man's whistle, determined, and somewhat aggressive. Sylvia left the cow and stepped aside into the bushes, but she was just too late. The man had discovered her, and called out in a very cheerful and persuasive tone, "Halloa, little girl, how far is it to the road?" and trembling Sylvia answered almost inaudibly, "A good ways."

She did not dare to look boldly at the tall young man, who carried a gun over his shoulder, but she came out of her bush and again followed the cow, while he walked alongside.

"I have been hunting for some birds." the stranger said kindly, "and I have lost my way, and need a friend very much. Don't be afraid." he added gallantly. "Speak up and tell me what your name is, and whether you think I can spend the night at your house, and go out gunning early in the morning."

Sylvia was more alarmed than before. Would not her grandmother consider her much to blame? But who could have foreseen such an accident as this? It did not appear to be her fault, and she hung her head as if the stem of it were broken,[4] but managed to answer "Sylvy", with much effort when the man again asked her name.

---

4) 머리 기둥이 부러진 듯 고개를 떨궜다.

5 Mrs. Tilley was standing in the doorway when the trio[5] came into view. The cow gave a loud moo by way of explanation.

"Yes, you'd better speak up for yourself, you old trial![6] Where'd she hid herself away this time, Sylvy?" Sylvia kept an awed silence; she knew by instinct that her grandmother did not comprehend the gravity of the situation. She must be mistaking the stranger for one of the farmer-lads of the region.

The young man stood his gun beside the door, and dropped a heavy game-bag beside it; then he bade Mrs. Tilley good-evening, and repeated his wayfarer's story, and asked if he could have a night's lodging.

"Put me anywhere you like." he said. "I must be off early in the morning, before day; but I am very hungry, indeed. You can give me some milk at any rate, that's plain."

"Dear sakes, yes." responded the hostess, whose long slumbering hospitality seemed to be easily awakened. "You might fare better if you went out on the main road a mile or so, but you're welcome to what we've got. I'll milk right off, and you make yourself at home. You can sleep on husks or feathers." she said graciously. "I raised them all myself. There's good pasturing for geese just below here towards the marsh. Now step round and set a plate for the gentleman, Sylvy!" And

---

5) Sylvia, the cow, and the man.
6) you old trial 늙은 골칫거리[소]야.

Sylvia promptly stepped. She was glad to have something to do, and she was hungry herself.

6 It was a surprise to find so clean and comfortable a little dwelling in this New England wilderness.[7] The young man had known the horrors of its most primitive housekeeping, and the dreary squalor of that level of society which does not rebel at the companionship of hens.[8] This house was the best old-fashioned farmstead he had ever seen. He listened eagerly to the old woman's quaint talk,[9] he watched Sylvia's pale face and shining gray eyes with ever growing enthusiasm, and insisted that this was the best supper he had eaten for a month; then, afterward, the new-made friends[10] sat down in the doorway together while the moon came up.

7 "Soon it would be berry-time, and Sylvia was a great help at picking. The cow was a good milker, though a plaguey thing to keep track of." the hostess gossiped frankly, adding that she had buried four children, so that Sylvia's mother, and a son in California were all the children she had left. "Dan, my boy, was

---

7) wilderness: 삼림지역.
8) 뉴잉글랜드[미국 북동부] 시골의 원시적인 살림살이, 그리고 닭과 함께 지내는 것을 마다하지 않는
   그런 시골 사회의 끔찍한 궁핍함을 이 젊은이는 익히 알고 있었던 터/하지만 실비아의 집은 달랐다
9) quaint talk: 뉴잉글랜드 시골의 사투리가 섞인 기이한 말투.
10) Sylvia, the grandmother, and the man.

a great hand to go gunning." she explained sadly. "I never wanted for patridges[11] or gray squirrels while he was to home. He's been a great hunter."

"Sylvia takes after him." the grandmother continued affectionately, after a minute's pause. "There ain't a foot o'[12] ground she don't know her way over, and the wild creatures count on her o' themselves.[13] She'll tame squirrels to come an'[14] feed right out o'[15] her hands, and all sorts o' birds. Last winter she got the jay-birds here, and I believe she'd 'a[16] scanted herself of her own meals to have plenty to throw out amongst 'em, if I hadn't kep' watch.[17]

8 "So Sylvy knows all about birds, does she?" the man exclaimed, as he looked round at Sylvia who sat in the moonlight. "I am making a collection of birds myself. I have been at it ever since I was a boy." he said. "There are two or three very rare ones I have been hunting for these five years. I mean to get them on my own ground if they can be found."

---

11) partridges(자고새)의 사투리.

12) on의 사투리.

13) 실비아는 숲길을 모조리 다 알며, 야생동물들도 실비아를 믿는다. (o' 등 다양한 사투리들이 구사되고 있음)

14) and의 사투리.

15) of의 사투리.

16) have의 사투리.

17) 내가 감시하지 않으면 야생동물들에게 자기 음식을 다 줘 버릴 것이다.

"Do you cage 'em up?" asked Mrs. Tilley doubtfully, in response to this enthusiastic announcement of the man.

"Oh, no, they're stuffed and preserved,[18] dozens and dozens of them." said the man, "and I have shot or snared every one myself. I caught a glimpse of a white heron three miles from here on Saturday, and I have followed it in this direction. They have never been found in this district at all. The little white heron, it is." and he turned again to look at Sylvia with the hope of discovering that the rare bird was one of her acquaintances.

But Sylvia was watching a toad in the narrow footpath.

"You would know the heron if you saw it." the stranger continued eagerly. "A queer tall white bird with soft feathers and long thin legs. And it would have a nest perhaps in the top of a high tree, made of sticks, something like a hawk's nest."

9   Sylvia's heart gave a wild beat; she knew that strange white bird, and had once stolen[19] softly near where it stood in some bright green swamp grass, away over at the other side of the woods. There was an open place where the sunshine always seemed strangely yellow and hot, where tall, nodding rushes grew, and her grandmother had warned her that she might sink in the soft black mud underneath and never be heard of more.

---

18) 박제시켜 보관한다.
19) 살금살금 몰래 다가가다.

Not far beyond were the salt marshes and beyond those was the sea, the sea which Sylvia wondered and dreamed about, but never had looked upon, though its great sound could often be heard on stormy nights.

"I can't think of anything I should like so much as to find that heron's nest." the man was saying. "I would give ten dollars to anybody who could show it to me." he added desperately, "and I mean to spend my whole vacation hunting for it if necessary."

Mrs. Tilley gave amazed attention to all this, but Sylvia still watched the toad and thought how many wished-for treasures the ten dollars would buy.

10 The next day the young man hovered about the woods, and Sylvia kept him company. Now her first fear of the man was gone, for he proved to be most kind and sympathetic. He told her many things about the birds and what they knew and where they lived and what they did with themselves. And he gave her a jack-knife, which she thought as great a treasure as if she were a desert-islander. All day long he did not once make her troubled or afraid except when he shot down some birds unexpectedly. Sylvia thought she would have liked him better without his gun; she could not understand why he killed the very birds he seemed to like so much. But as the day waned, Sylvia still watched the young man with loving admiration. She

had never seen anybody so charming and delightful; the woman's heart, asleep in the girl, was vaguely thrilled by a dream of love. Some premonition of that great power stirred and swayed these young foresters who traversed the solemn woodlands with soft-footed silent care. They stopped to listen to a bird's song; they pressed forward again eagerly, parting the branches, speaking to each other rarely and in whispers; the young man going first and Sylvia following, a few steps behind, with her gray eyes dark with excitement.

She felt sorry for the white heron not to be found, but she did not lead the man to find it, either. She only followed. At last evening began to fall, and they drove the cow home together, and Sylvia smiled with pleasure when they came to the place where she heard the whistle and was afraid only the night before.

$$\boxed{\text{II}}$$

11 Half a mile from home, at the farther edge of the woods, where the land was highest, a great pine-tree stood. Whether it was left for a boundary mark,[20] or for what reason, no one could say; the woodchoppers who had fell its mates[21] were

---

20) 어떤 경계를 표시하기 위해 심어 둔 나무인지.

dead and gone long ago, and a whole forest of sturdy trees, pines and oaks and maples, had grown again. But the stately head of this old pine towered above them all and made a landmark for sea and shore miles and miles away. Sylvia knew it well. She had always believed that whoever climbed to the top of it could see the ocean; and she had often laid her hand on the great rough trunk and looked up wistfully at those dark boughs that the wind always stirred, no matter how hot and still the air might be below. Now she thought of the tree with a new excitement. She thought if one climbed the tree at break of day, he could see all the world, and easily discover where the white heron flew, and mark the place, and find the hidden nest. What a spirit of adventure, what wild ambition! What fancied triumph and delight and glory for the later morning when she could find the secret! It was too great for her heart to bear.

All night the door of the little house stood open, and the whippoorwills came and sang upon the step. The young man and the old hostess were sound asleep, but Sylvia's great design kept her broad awake and watching. She forgot to think of sleep. The short summer night seemed as long as the winter night, and at last when the whippoorwills ceased. Sylvia stole[22] out of the house and followed the pasture path through the

---

21) 친구 나무들, 즉 주변의 나무들을 베어 낸 나무꾼/ it은 키 큰 소나무.
22) 몰래 나오다.

woods, hastening toward the open ground beyond, listening with a sense of comfort and companionship to the drowsy twitter of a half-awakened bird, whose perch she had jarred in passing.

There was the huge tree asleep yet in the paling moonlight, and small and hopeful Sylvia began with utmost bravery to mount to the top of it, with eager blood coursing the channels of her whole frame, with her bare feet and fingers. The huge pine tree seemed to reach up, up, almost to the sky itself. First she must mount the white oak tree that grew alongside, where she was almost lost among the dark branches and the green leaves heavy and wet with dew; a bird fluttered off its nest, and a red squirrel ran to and fro and scolded pettishly at the harmless housebreaker.23) Sylvia felt her way easily. She had often climbed there, and knew that one of the oak's upper branches chafed against the pine trunk. There, when she made the dangerous pass from one tree to the other, the great adventure would really begin.

She crept out along the swaying oak tree branch at last, and took the daring step across into the old pine tree. The way was harder than she thought; she must reach far and hold fast, the sharp dry twigs caught and held her and scratched her like angry talons,24) the pitch25) made her thin fingers stiff as she

---

23) 주거침입자, 즉 실비아.
24) 맹금.

went round and round the tree's huge trunk, higher and higher upward. The sparrows and robins in the woods below were beginning to wake and twitter to the dawn, yet it seemed much lighter there aloft in the pine tree,26) and Sylvia knew that she must hurry if her project were to be successful.

12 The tree seemed to lengthen itself out as she went up, and to reach farther and farther upward.27) It was like a great main-mast to the voyaging earth.28) The tree must truly have been amazed that morning as this determined spark of human spirit29) crept and climbed from branch to branch high in the air. Who knows how steadily the twigs held themselves to advantage this weak creature30) on her way! The old pine must have loved this creature more than all the hawks, and bats, and moths, and even the sweet-voiced thrushes. And the tree stood still and held away the winds that June morning while the dawn grew bright in the east.

---

25) pitch: height, 즉 나무의 까마득한 높이 때문에 기온이 내려가고 손가락이 뻣뻣함.
26) 아래는 아직 희미한 새벽이지만 높은 나무 위에서는 벌써 빛이 밝게 비침.
27) 아무리 올라가도 마치 나무가 키가 더 커지는(lenghten) 것처럼 꼭대기까지 이르지 못함.
28) 마치 지구가 하나의 배이고 나무가 그 배에 꽂힌 돛과 같다고 비유함으로써 나무의 크기를 과장되게 표현함.
29) 실비아를 뜻함. 나무를 위대한 자연으로, 그 나무의 입장에서 실비아를 조그마하고 미숙한 생명체로 바라보는 상황으로 그려냄. 나무는 실비아를 대견하게 여기고 실비아의 모험이 성공할 수 있도록 자비롭게 돕고 있음.
30) 실비아를 뜻함.

Sylvia's face was like a pale star, if one had seen it from the ground.31) Finally when the last thorny bough was past, Sylvia stood trembling and tired, high in the tree-top. Yes, there was the sea with the dawning sun making a golden dazzle over it, and toward that glorious east flew two hawks with slow-moving pinions.32) How low they33) looked in the air from that height, and dark against the blue sky. Their gray feathers were as soft as moths; they seemed only a little way from the tree, and Sylvia felt as if she too could go flying away among the clouds. Westward, the woodlands and farms reached miles and miles into the distance; here and there were church steeples, and white villages; truly it was a vast and awesome world.

13 The birds sang louder and louder. At last the sun came up bewilderingly bright.34) Sylvia could see the white sails of ships out at sea, and the clouds that were purple and rose-colored and yellow. Where was the white heron's nest in the sea of green branches, and was this wonderful sight of the

---

31) 만약 지상에서 누군가 실비아를 봤으면 너무 높은 곳에 있어서 실비아가 하나의 작고 희미한 (pale) 별처럼 보였을 것이다.

32) 두 마리의 매가 천천히 움직이는 날개를 하고 일출로 빛나는 동쪽 하늘로 날아가고 있음. toward that glorious east flew two hawks with slow-moving pinions는 도치문장으로 two hawks with slow-moving pinions flew toward that glorious east.

33) two hawks 여기서는 큰 매(hawk)도 소나무의 높이에서는 저 아래로 작게 보임. 이하 몇 문장의 they는 모두 hawks를 칭함.

34) 눈을 멀게 하듯이 강렬하게 햇빛이 비치기 시작함.

world the only reward for having climbed to such a giddy height?[35]) Now look down again, Sylvia, where the green marsh is set among the shining birches and dark hemlocks; there where you saw the white heron once you will see him again; look, look! a white spot of him like a single floating feather comes up from the dead hemlock and grows larger, and rises, and comes close at last, and goes by the pine tree with steady sweep of wing and outstretched slender neck and crested head. And wait! wait! do not move a foot or a finger, little girl, do not send an arrow of light and consciousness from your two eager eyes, for the heron has perched on a pine bough not far beyond yours, and cries back to his mate on the nest, and plumes his feathers for the new day!

Sylvia gives a long sigh a minute later when a company of shouting cat-birds comes also to the tree, and being vexed by their fluttering and lawlessness the solemn heron goes away.[36]) She knows his secret now, the wild, light, slender bird that floats and wavers, and goes back like an arrow presently to his home in the green world beneath. Then Sylvia, well satisfied,

---

35) 이탤릭 부분은 작가의 개입. 갑자기 전지적 시점을 깨고 작가가 직접 목소리를 내는 부분으로 처음에는 비평가들의 비난을 많이 받았음. 그러나 오히려 현장의 직접성을 강조하고 실비아에 대한 작가의 애정과 격려, 그리고 white heron이 떠오르는 모습을 생생하게 전달한다는 점에서 효과적인 일탈로 그 평가가 달라졌음. 시제 역시 일관성을 깨고 현재 시제를 사용함으로써 극적 효과가 배가 됨.

36) 캣버드들의 시끄러움 때문에 vexed되어서 white heron이 나무에 앉아있다 날아가 버림. 그래서 실비아가 아쉬움의 한숨을 쉬는 대목. a company of shouting cat-birds: 한 무리의 캣버드들. being vexed by their fluttering and lawlessness은 분사구문: 캣버드들의 퍼덕임과 무질서함에 정신이 산란해져서.

makes her perilous way down again,[37] not daring to look far below the branch she stands on, ready to cry sometimes because her fingers ache and her lamed feet slip.

14 "Sylvy, Sylvy!" called the old grandmother again and again, but nobody answered, and the small husk bed was empty, and Sylvia had disappeared.

The guest waked from a dream, and remembering his day's pleasure hurried to dress himself. He was sure from the way the shy little girl looked yesterday that she had at least seen the white heron,[38] and now she must really be persuaded to tell. Here she comes now, paler than ever, and her worn old frock is torn and tattered, and smeared with pine pitch. The grandmother and the man stand in the door together and question her.

But Sylvia does not speak after all, though the grandmother rebukes her, and the young man looks straight in her eyes with his kind appealing eyes. He says he can make her rich with money; he has promised it. Now he waits to hear the story she can tell.

No, she must keep silence! What is it that suddenly makes her keep silent? Now, when the great luck for the first time

---

37) 나무를 위태위태하게 내려온다.
38) 어제 실비아가 하던 것으로 보아 white heron의 소재를 알고 있음을 확신했다.

puts out a hand to her, must she thrust it aside for a bird's sake?[39] The murmur of the pine's green branches is in her ears, she remembers how the white heron came flying through the golden air and how they watched the sea and the morning together, and Sylvia cannot speak; she cannot tell the heron's secret and give its life away.

Sylvia felt a sharp pang as the man went away later in the day! Many a night Sylvia heard the echo of his whistle haunting the pasture path as she came home with the cow. She forgot her sorrow at the sharp sound of his gun and at the poor sight of thrushes and sparrows dropping silent to the ground,[40] their songs hushed and their pretty feathers stained and wet with blood. Were the birds better friends than their hunter might have been, — who can tell? Woodlands and summer-time, remember what treasures she lost![41] Bring your gifts and graces and tell your secrets to this lonely country child!

---

39) 새 한 마리 때문에 처음으로 들어 온 행운을 포기해야 하는가?
40) 사냥꾼의 날카로운 총소리를 듣거나 총에 맞아 떨어진 찌바귀새나 참새들을 보았을 때 사냥꾼이 떠나간 사실에서 느끼는 슬픈 감정이 사라져 버림.
41) 여기서부터는 작가가 직접 자연에게 말을 걸어, 자연을 위해 실비아가 연정과 재산을 포기하였으니 그에 대한 대가로 귀한 선물을 내려주기를 요청함.

Comprehension Check-Up Questions

1. Why did Sylvia look upon the cow as a playmate? (section 1)

2. How does Sylvia feel about living on the farm? (section 2)

3. What sound surprises Sylvia in the woods? Why is she "horror-stricken" to hear this sound? (section 4)

4. Why is Sylvia alarmed? (section 4)

5. In what is the guest interested? (section 8)

6. Why has the young man come to the district where Sylvia and her grandmother live? (section 8)

7. How does Sylvia feel about the young man killing birds? (section 10)

8. Is Sylvia hoping to help find the white heron? (section 10)

9. What keeps Sylvia awake? (section 11)

10. What "day's pleasure" is the young man anticipating? (section 14)

11. What does Sylvia do about telling the location of the white heron's nest? (section 14)

I Stand Here Ironing

Tillie Olsen

Tillie Lerner Olsen (1912–2007) was an American writer associated with the political turmoil of the 1930s and the first generation of American feminists. Olsen was born to Russian Jewish immigrants in Wahoo, Nebraska and moved to Omaha while a young child. There she attended Lake School in the Near North Side through the eighth grade, living among the city's Jewish community. At age 15, she dropped out of Omaha High School to enter the work force. Over the years Olsen worked as a waitress, domestic worker, and meat trimmer. She was also a union organizer and political activist in the Socialist community. In 1932, Olsen began to write her first novel *Yonnondio*, the same year she gave birth to Karla, the first of four daughters. In 1933, Olsen moved to California where she continued her union activities. In the 1930s she joined the American Communist party. She was briefly jailed in 1934 while organizing a packing house workers' union (the charge was "making loud and unusual noise"), an experience she wrote about in *The Nation, The New Republic, and The Partisan Review.* She later moved to San Francisco, California, where in 1936 she met and lived with Jack Olsen, who was an organizer and a longshoreman. In 1937, she gave birth to her second child, her first child with her future husband Jack Olsen, whom she married in 1944, on the eve of his departure for service in World War II. San Francisco remained her home until her 85th year when she moved to Berkeley, California, to a cottage behind the home of her youngest daughter. Olsen died on January 1, 2007, in Oakland, California, aged 94.

"I Stand Here Ironing" is a story anthologized in *Tell Me a Riddle* (1961). The book is a collection of four short stories, most linked by the characters in one family. Three of the stories were from the point of view of mothers. "I Stand Here Ironing" is the first and shortest story in the collection, about a woman who is grieving about her daughter's life and about the circumstances that shaped her own mothering. "O Yes" is the story of a white woman whose young daughter's friendship with a black girl is narrowed and ended by the pressures of junior high school. "Hey Sailor, What Ship?" is told by an aging merchant marine sailor whose friendship with a San Francisco family (relatives of the main character in "Tell Me a Riddle") is becoming increasingly strained due to his alcoholism. (In later editions of the book, "Hey Sailor, What Ship?" appears as the second story in the collection). All four stories in Tell Me a Riddle were featured in Best American Short Stories, in the year each was first published in a literary magazine. The title story was awarded the O. Henry Award in 1961 for best American short story. "I Stand Here Ironing" is a story about guilt, guilt that will be developed during the narration of the whole story. The mother is standing here ironing and within the next 30 minutes she will recall the whole trip of her and her daughter's life (*adapted from Wikipedia*).

fierce rigidity of first motherhood

batter

decree

shining bubbles of sound

overall

ecstasy

blur

clogged weeping

chicken pox

shoddy red

shoddy red

fatigue

laceration

curdle

hunch

scaredy

clutch and implore

the explosions, the tempers,

the denunciation, the demand

moan or restless stirring

convalescent home

sleek

gigantic red bows

ravaged looks

unless otherwise notified

contaminate

parental germs

labored writing

personal possessions

plead

frailer

runny eggs

mush with lumps

stay stiff

twinkling by

fret

glib or quick

over-conscientious

strictness about attendance

asthma

1 I stand here ironing, and what you asked me moves tormented back and forth with the iron.

"I wish you would manage the time to come in and talk with me about your daughter. I'm sure you can help me understand her. She's a youngster who needs help and whom I'm deeply interested in helping."

Emily really needs help? Even if I came, what good would it do?[1] You think because I am her mother I have a key, or that in some way you could use me as a key. She has lived for nineteen years and all that life has happened outside of me, beyond me.

And when is there time to remember, to sift, to weigh, to estimate, to total?[2] I will start and there will be an interruption and I will have to gather it all together again. Or I will become engulfed with all I did or did not do, with what should have been and what cannot be helped.[3]

2 She was a beautiful baby. The first and only one of our five[4] that was beautiful at birth. I nursed her.[5] I nursed all the children, but with her, with all the fierce rigidity of first motherhood. I did as the books then said.[6] Though her cries

---

1) 내가 학교에 간다 해도 무슨 소용 있겠어요?
2) 언제 과거일을 기억하여 찬찬히 살펴보고, 무게를 달고, 판단하고, 종합할만한 그런 시간이나 있었던가요? 너무 바빠 지금처럼 에밀리의 지난 일을 회상할 시간도 없었다는 뜻.
3) 이제 과거 일을 회상을 한 번 해보려 함. 혹시 중간에 다른 집안일로 회상이 끊길 때가 있기도 할 텐데 그 때는 다시 앞의 회상을 다시 복원해야 할 것. 혹은 내가 과거에 했던 일들과 내가 하지 못했던 일들, 했어야만 했던 일과 어찌 할 수 없었던 일들이 새삼스럽게 다시 나를 엄습해 버릴 수도 있을 것임.
4) five: five children
5) 모유수유해서 키우다.
6) 육아책에 적혀있는 대로 하였다.

battered me to trembling and my breasts ached with swollenness, I waited till the clock decreed.

Why do I put that first? I do not even know if it matters, or if it explains anything.[7]

She was a beautiful baby. She blew shining bubbles of sound. She loved motion, loved light, loved color and music and textures. She would lie on the floor in her blue overalls patting the surface so hard in ecstasy her hands and feet would blur. She was a miracle to me, but when she was eight months old I had to leave her daytimes with the woman downstairs to whom she was no miracle at all, for I worked in stead of Emily's father, who "could no longer endure" (he wrote in his goodbye note) "sharing want with us."[8]

I was nineteen. It was the pre-relief world of the depression.[9] I would[10] start running as soon as I got off the streetcar, running up the stairs, the place smelling sour. When she saw me Emily would break into a clogged weeping that could not be comforted, a weeping I can hear yet.

After a while I found a job at night so I could be with her days, and it was better. But a little later I could not afford to take care

---

7) 어떻게 이야기를 풀어가야 하는지. 무슨 말부터 해야 하는지. 설명 자체가 무슨 의미가 있는지 . . .
8) 가난을 견디지 못해 떠난다고 쪽지를 써놓고 가출했던 남편. 여기서 want=poverty.
9) 대공황으로 인해 사회복지기금제도가 마련되던 이전의 시기 사람이어서 사회보장의 혜택을 받지 못함.
10) 이하 would는 과거의 불규칙한 습관을 나타내는 조동사.

of her again and had to bring her to his family[11] and leave her.

It took a long time to raise the money to get her back. Then she got chicken pox and I had to wait longer. When she finally came, I hardly knew her, walking quick and nervous like her father, looking like her father, thin, and dressed in a shoddy red that yellowed her skin and glared at the pockmarks. All the baby loveliness gone.

She was two. Old enough for nursery school they[12] said, and I did not know then what I know now ____ the fatigue of the long day, and the lacerations of group life in the kinds of nurseries that are only parking places for children.[13]

Except that it would have made no difference if I had known.[14] It was the only place there was. It was the only way we could be together, the only way I could hold a job.

The teacher there was evil. All these years it has curdled into my memory: the little boy hunched in the corner and she yelled, "why aren't you outside, because Alvin hits you? that's no reason, go out, scaredy." I knew Emily hated the nursery school even if she did not clutch and implore "don't go

---

11) 남편의 가족, 즉 에밀리의 친가.
12) 에밀리를 어린이집에 보내기를 권하는 이웃사람들.
13) ____ 이하는 what I know now의 내용. 하루 종일 어린이 집에 있는 것이 얼마나 피곤한 것인지 또 아이들을 주차장처럼 맡겨놓는 어린이 집에서 집단 생활을 하는 것이 얼마나 깊이 상처를 받는 것인지. laceration은 깊이 찢음, 그 결과로 난 상처, 열상.
14) 어린이집이 그런 곳이라는 것을 알았다 하더라도 보낼 수밖에 없는 상황.

Mommy" like the other children, mornings.

She always had a reason why we should stay home. Momma, you look sick, Momma, I feel sick. Momma, the teachers aren't there today, they're sick. Momma, we can't go, there was a fire there last night. Momma, it's a holiday today, no school, they told me.

But never a direct protest, never rebellion. I think of my other children in their three, four-year-oldness ____ the explosions, the tempers, the denunciations, the demands ____ and I feel suddenly ill. I put the iron down.15) What in me demanded that goodness in her? And what was the cost, the cost to her of such goodness?

3 The old man living in the back once said in his gentle way: "You should smile at Emily more when you look at her." What was in my face when I looked at her? I loved her. There were all the acts of love.

It was only with the other kids I understood what he said,16) and it was the face of joy, and not of care or tightness or worry I turned to them ____ too late for Emily. She does not smile easily, as her brothers and sisters do. Her face is closed and

---

15) 과거의 기억이 너무 사무쳐 다림질을 잠깐 쉬는 장면.
16) 에밀의 동생들을 키우면서 비로소 그 노인이 말한 뜻을 이해하게 되었다. it . . . that 강조 용법.
  여기서는 that이 생략됨.

sombre, but when she wants, how fluid.17) You18) must have seen it in her pantomimes, you spoke of her rare gift for comedy on the stage that rouses a laughter out of the audience so dear they applaud and applaud and do not want to let her go.

4 Where does it come from, that comedy? There was none of it19) in her when she came back to me that second time, after I had had to send her away again.20) She had a new daddy now to learn to love, and I think perhaps it was a better time.

Sometimes my husband and I left her alone nights, telling ourselves she was old enough.

"Can't you go some other time, Mommy, like tomorrow?" she would ask. "Will it be just a little while you'll be gone? Do you promise?"

The time we came back, the front door was wide open and the clock was on the floor in the hall. She was rigid awake. "It wasn't just a little while. I didn't cry. Three times I called you,

---

17) 의도할 때는 얼마나 유동적인지. 즉 웃고자 할 때는 굳었던 얼굴이 완전히 풀림. 에밀리의 우울한 표정은 따라서 천성적이라기 보다는 양육 방식의 결과.

18) You=선생님.

19) it=comedy. 에밀리가 화자의 재혼으로 다시 두 번째로 화자의 곁을 떠나 convalescent home에서 생활하게 되고(이 이야기는 조금 있다가 화자의 독백으로 전개됨) 거기서 일정 기간 을 지나 다시 집에 오게 되었을 때 그 때 에밀리의 얼굴에는 웃음기라고는 없었다. 이하 에밀리가 그곳으로 보내진 경위 및 결과가 회상됨.

20) 에밀리를 다시 사정상 다른 곳으로 떼어 놓았음. 그리고 에밀리가 다시 돌아올 무렵 화자는 재혼, 에밀리는 이제 새아버지가 생김.

just three times, and then I ran downstairs to open the door so you could come faster. The clock talked loud. I threw it away, it scared me ___ what it talked."21)

She said the clock talked loud again that night I went to the hospital to have Susan.22) Emily was delirious with the fever that comes before red measles, but she was fully conscious all the week when I was gone and the week after we were home when she could not come near the new baby or me.

She did not get well. She stayed skeleton thin,23) not wanting to eat. Night after night she had nightmares. She would call for me, and I would rouse from exhaustion and sleepily called back: "You're all right, darling, go to sleep, it's just a dream." and if she still called, I called out in a sterner voice, "now go to sleep, Emily, there's nothing to hurt you." Twice, only twice, when I had to get up for Susan anyhow, I went in to sit with her.

Now24) when it is too late, I get up and go to her at once at her moan or restless stirring. "Are you awake, Emily? Can I get you something?" And the answer is always the same: "No, I'm all right, go back to sleep, Mother."

They25) persuaded me at the clinic to send her away to a

---

21) What it talked. 시계가 알려주는 것, 즉 한밤중 시간이어서 무서움.
22) 에밀리의 동생.
23) 해골처럼 비쩍 말랐다.
24) 에밀리가 다 큰 시점인 현재, 너무 늦어버린 현재에서야 에밀리에게 다가감.
25) They=일반사람들, 여기서는 병원관련자들.

convalescent home in the country where "she can have the kind of food and care you can't manage for her, and you'll be free to concentrate on the new baby." They still send children to that place. I see pictures on the society page of sleek young women planning affairs to raise money for it, or dancing at the affairs, or decorating Easter eggs or filling Christmas stockings for the children.

They never have a picture of the children so I do not know if the girls still wear those gigantic red bows and the ravaged looks on the every other Sunday when parents can come to visit "unless otherwise notified" ___ as we were notified the first six weeks.[26]

Oh the convalescent home was a handsome place with green lawns and tall trees and flower beds. High up on the balconies of each cottage[27] the children stood, the girls in their red bows and white dresses, the boys in white suits and giant red ties. The parents stood below shrieking up to be heard and the children shrieked down to be heard, and between them the invisible wall "Not To Be Contaminated by Parental Germs or Physical Affection."

---

26) "다른 안내가 없으면" 격주 방문 허용함. 첫 6주는 계속 방문하지 말라는 안내문이 와서 면회를 하지 못함.
27) 각 병동(cottage: 여기서 cottage는 작은 별도 건물을 뜻함. 아이들의 건강 상태에 따라 각각 다른 cottage에 수용)의 발코니 위로 높이 올라 선 상태에서 아이들은 저 멀리 아래에 위치한 부모와 면회.

She wrote once a week, the labored writing of a seven-year-old. "I am fine. How is the baby. If I write my leter nicly28) I will have a star. Love." She never had a star yet. We wrote every other day, letters she could never hold or keep but only hear read ___ once.29) "We simply do not have room for children to keep any personal possessions." they just replied when we pleaded how much it would mean to Emily to be allowed to keep her letters and cards.

Each visit she looked frailer. "She isn't eating." they told us.

(They had runny eggs for breakfast or mush with lumps, Emily said later, I'd hold it in my mouth and not swallow.)

It took us eight months to get her back home. I tried to hold and love her after she came back, but her body would stay stiff, and after a while she'd push away. She ate little. Food sickened her, and I think much of life, too.30) Oh she had physical lightness and brightness, twinkling by on skates, bouncing like a ball up and down up and down over the jump rope, skimming over the hill; but these were momentary.

5   She fretted about her appearance, thin and dark and foreign-looking at a time when every little girl was supposed to

---

28) letter nicely를 틀리게 쓴 것.
29) 편지를 갖지 못하게 할 뿐만 아니라 한 번만 얼른 에밀리에게 읽어주고 만 병원측. once는 딱 한 번으로 대시 처리를 통해 강조.
30) Food sickened her, and I think much of life sickened her, too.

look or thought she should look a chubby blonde replica of Shirley Temple.[31] The doorbell sometimes rang for her, but no one seemed to come and play in the house or be a best friend. Maybe because we moved so much.

There was a boy she loved painfully through two school semesters. Months later she told me how she had taken pennies from my purse to buy him candy. "Licorice was his favorite and I brought him some every day, but he still liked Jennifer better' n me. Why, Mommy?" The kind of question for which there is no answer.

School was a worry to her. She was not glib or quick in a world where glibness and quickness were easily confused with ability to learn. To her overworked and exasperated teachers she was an over-conscientious "slow learner" who kept trying to catch up and was absent too often.

I let her be absent, though sometimes the illness was imaginary.[32] How different from my now ____ strictness about attendance with the other children. I wasn't working then. We had a new baby, I was home anyhow. Sometimes, after Susan grew old enough. I would[33] keep her home from school, too, to have them all together. Mostly Emily had asthma, and her

---

31) 당시 유명한 아역 배우. 이후 미국 여성 어린이의 미의 전형으로 찬미되면서 인형 및 각종 디자인에 상업적으로 이용됨.
32) 상상으로 아픈 때에도, 즉 몸이 실제 아프지 않을 때 결석해도 모른 척 해 버림.
33) 이하 would는 과거의 습관.

breathing, harsh and labored, would fill the house with a curiously tranquil sound. I would brought boxes of collections to her bed. She would select beads and single earrings, bottle tops and shells, dried flowers and pebbles, old postcards and scraps, all sorts of oddments; then she and Susan would play Kingdom, setting up landscapes and furniture, peopling them with action.

Oh there are conflicts between the other children, needing, demanding, hurting, taking ____ but only between Emily and Susan, no. Susan, the second child, Susan, golden, and curly-haired and chubby, quick and articulate and assured, everything in appearance and manner Emily was not; Susan, so anxious to hold Emily's precious things, losing or sometimes clumsily breaking them; Susan telling jokes and riddles to company for applause while Emily sat silent (Emily said to me later: that was my riddle, Mother, I told it to Susan); Susan, who for all the five years' difference in age was just a year behind Emily in developing physically.

Ronnie is calling.34) He is wet35) and I change him. It is rare there is such a cry now. That time of motherhood is almost behind me when the ear is not one's own but must always be racked and listening for the child cry and call. We36) sit for a

---

34) 에밀리 이야기를 하던 중 갑자기 막내아들 Ronni의 울음소리가 들려옴. 시간은 과거에서 현재로.
35) 기저귀가 젖음.

while and I hold him, looking out over the city spread in charcoal with its soft aisles of light. "Shoogily"[37] he breathes and curls closer. I carry him back to bed, asleep. Shoogily. A funny word, a family word, inherited from Emily, invented by her to say: comfort.

6 In this and other ways she leaves her seal, I say aloud. And startle at my saying it. What do I mean? I was at the terrible, growing years.[38] War years. I do not remember them well. I was working, there were four smaller ones, there was no time for her. She had to help be a mother, and housekeeper, and shopper. Mornings of crisis and near hysteria trying to get lunches packed, hair combed, coats and shoes found, everyone to school or Child Care on time, the baby ready for transportation. And always the paper scribbled on by a smaller one, the book looked at by Susan then mislaid, the homework not done.[39] Running out to that huge school where she was one, she was lost, she was a drop; suffering over the unpreparedness, stammering and unsure in her classes.

There was so little time left at night after the kids were

---

36) 화자와 Ronnie.
37) 이어 설명되는 것처럼 에밀리가 가족을 즐겁게 해주려고 만든 일종의 의성어.
38) 아이 양육으로 매우 힘들었던 때. 이어서 그 때를 전쟁으로 묘사함(War years).
39) 에밀리의 학교 종이는 동생이 낙서를 하고, 책은 Susan이 보고는 어디론가 못 찾는 곳에 놓아두고, 숙제는 못한 상태. 에밀리의 등교 장면임.

bedded down. She would struggle over books, and I would be ironing, or preparing food for the next day, or writing a mail to Bill[40], or tending the baby. Sometimes, to make me laugh, or out of her despair, she would imitate happenings at school.

I think I said once: "Why don't you do something like this in the school amateur show?" One morning she phoned me at work, hardly understandable through the weeping: "Mother, I did it. I won, I won; they gave me first prize; they clapped and clapped and wouldn't let me go."

Now suddenly she was Somebody.[41] She began to be asked to perform at other high schools, even in colleges, then at city and statewide affairs. The first one we went to and I barely recognized her because she looked too thin: she looked almost drowned herself into the curtains. Then: Was this Emily? The control, the command, the convulsing and deadly clowning, the spell, then the roaring, stamping audience, unwilling to let this rare and precious laughter out of their lives.

Afterwards:[42] You ought to do something about her with a gift like that ____ but without money or knowing how, what can I do? We have left it all to her, and the gift has as often eddied

---

40) 2차대전에 참전 중이던 남편 빌에게 편지를 씀.
41) Somebody, 유명인사. 이제 팬터마임으로 학교에서뿐만 아니라 여러 다른 곳에 초대될 정도로 유명인이 됨. 에밀리의 현재로 이야기가 비약함.
42) 학교 선생님의 편지로 다시 생각이 옮겨감. Afterwards: You ought to do something about her with a gift like that 는 편지의 마지막 추신 부분.

inside, clogged and clotted, as been used and growing. She is coming[43]. She runs up the stairs two at a time with her light graceful step, and I know she is happy tonight.

"Aren't you ever going to finish the ironing, Mother? Whistler[44] painted his mother in a rocker. I'd have to paint mine standing over an ironing board." This is one of her communicative nights and she tells me everything and nothing[45] as she fixes herself a plate of food out of the icebox. She is so lovely.

She starts up the stairs to bed. "Don't get me up in the morning.", "But I thought you were having midterms.", "Oh, those." she comes back in, kisses me, and says quite lightly, "in a couple of years when we'll all be atom dead they won't matter a bit."[46]

She has said it before. She believes it. But because I have been dredging the past, and all that compounds a human being is so heavy and meaningful in me, I cannot endure it tonight.

I will never total it all. I will never come in to say: She was a child seldom smiled at. Her father left me before she was a year old. I had to work her first six years when there was work, or I sent her to the relatives. There were years she hated. She was dark and thin and foreign-looking in a world where the

---

43) 선생님에게 독백을 하는 동안 에밀리가 학교에서 돌아옴.
44) 에밀리의 친구.
45) everything and nothing 크고 작은 온갖 일들.
46) 에밀리의 농담. 곧 원폭으로 멸망할 텐데 시험(they)이 무슨 문제래요?

prestige went to blondeness and curly hair and dimples. She was slow where glibness was prized. She was a child of anxious love, not proud one. We were poor and could not afford her the soil of easy growth. I was a young mother, I was a distracted mother. There were the other children pushing up, demanding. Her younger sister seemed all that she was not. There were years she did not want me to touch her. She kept too much in herself. She is a child of her age, of depression, of war, of fear.

Let her be.[47] So all that is in her will not bloom ___ but in how many does it?[48] There is still enough left to live by. Only help her to know that she is more than this dress on the ironing board, helpless before the iron.

---

47) 그러니 부질없이 에밀리를 도와준다 어쩐다 하지 말고 그냥 그 아이로 하여금 자기 길을 가도록 해 줍시다. 선생님은 에밀리의 재능이 활짝 피어나도록 돕자고 하지만.
48) 그렇게 하면 물론 에밀리의 잠재력이 다 피어나지 않을 수도 있다. 그러나 그렇게 100% 자신의 능력을 계발하는 사람들이 얼마나 될까?

Comprehension Check-Up Questions

1. What does the teacher ask the narrator for and why? (section 1)

2. How old is Emily now?

3. How does the mother respond to the letter?

4. Is this the first time for the mother to think about her daughter's life seriously? If so, why didn't she have such time before?

5. How pretty was Emily at birth and how did it change? (section 2)

6. What rules did the mother follow, when she raised her first baby, Emily?

7. Why did the husband leave home?

8. Who took care of the baby, while the mother was working in daytime?

9. How does the narrator remember when she came from work and saw Emily?

10. Why did the mother send Emily to her ex-husband's family? How did she change when she came back home after a while?

11. Where was Emily sent when she became 2? How was there?

12. How did Emily respond to her new place, nursery?

13. How differently does Emily change in her pantomimes? (section 3)

14. While the newly-weds were out at night, how did Emily spend time alone? (section 4)

15. When Emily had nightmares and asked her mother to stay with her, how did the mother respond and why? Now how does the mother fell about her past behaviors?

16. How was the convalescence home? Did Emily get better there? How long did shy stay there?

17. How different was Emily back home after the experiences at the institution?

18. How was Emily regarded by her teahers or mates? (section 5)

19. What kind of illness kept Emily from going to school?

20. Why did the mother have loose attitude toward Emily's absence?

21. Susan and Emily showed sharp contrast in many respects. How different were they?

Cathedral

Raymond Carver

Raymond Carver (1938–1988) grew up in Washington State. His father was a sawmill worker and his mother a waitress. Carver worked with his father in a sawmill in California and then as a deliveryman. He married his first wife, Maryann, and six months later a daughter was born. A son followed. Carver enrolled at various colleges, where his studies concentrated on creative writing. Aged twenty–two, "The Furious Seasons" ____ his first published story ____ appeared in college magazine Selection. "The Brass Ring" ____ his first published poem ____ appeared in 1962, in the little magazine *Targets*. In his late twenties, Carver filed for bankruptcy. His father died. He also got his first white collar job (textbook editor), and his story "Will You Please Be Quiet, Please?" appeared in The Best American Short Stories 1967.

Carver continued to move around, move jobs, and get stories and poems published. He began to lecture. He went bankrupt again and was hospitalized with acute alcoholism. In his late thirties, the stories *Will You Please Be Quiet, Please?* appeared ____ is first major press book. Carver stopped drinking. He met Tess Gallagher, and he and Maryann separated. The American Academy and Institute of Arts and Letters awarded him a fellowship to write full–time. At forty–nine, doctors diagnosed cancer.

They removed part of his left lung, but the cancer recurred. He had brain radiation treatment, but cancer reappeared. Ray and Tess married in Reno, on Friday 17 June 1988. He died at home, in Washington State, on 2 August. *(adapted from http://www.carversite.com)*

"**Cathedral**" is the title story of a collection published in 1983: *Cathedral*. "Cathedral" opens with the narrator telling the reader in a conversational tone that a blind friend of his wife's is coming to visit them. The narrator is clearly unhappy about the upcoming visit. He then flashes back to the story of how his wife met the blind man when she worked for him as a reader. Although his wife has maintained contact with the blind man for ten years, this will be the first time she has seen him since her marriage, subsequent divorce, and remarriage. The narrator's marriage with his wife suffers from lack of communication, which make both him and his wife feel very lonely. The narrator's anxiety increases while he observes the intimate and communicative relationship between his wife and Robert. Finally, the narrator is left with Robert and the television. The narrator attempts to describe what he sees on the television; however, when a cathedral appears in a documentary, the narrator is unable to find the words to describe it. Robert asks the narrator to get some paper and a pen so that they can draw a cathedral together. The drawing goes on and on. Finally, Robert tells the narrator to close his eyes and continue to draw. At this moment, something strange happens to the narrator (*adapted from Wikipedia*).

county social-service department

officer-to-be

commissioned officer

military-industrial thing

passed out

harmless chitchat

just as well

dish towel

insurance policy

pathetic

feature this

folks

look distinguished

heavy-set

spiffy

iris

pupil

socket

bub

Just a tad: Just a bit

nubbin

dope

numbers

toked v.

roach

pooped out

turn in

monopolize

disconcerting

drooped

skeleton costumes

pageant

precession

buttresses

countryside

interior stuff

droned on

1   This blind man, an old friend of my wife's, he was on his way to spend the night. His wife had died. So he was visiting the dead wife's relatives in Connecticut. He called my wife from his in-law's. Arrangements were made. He would come by train, a five-hour trip, and my wife would meet him at the station. She hadn't seen him since she worked for him on summer in Seattle ten years ago. But she and the blind man had kept in touch. They made tapes and mailed them back and forth. I wasn't enthusiastic about his visit. He was no one I knew. And his being blind bothered me. My idea of blindness came from the movies. In the movies, the blind moved slowly and never laughed. Sometimes they were led by seeing-eye dog. A blind man in my house was not something I looked forward to.

2   That summer in Seattle she had needed a job. She didn't have any money. The man she was going to marry at the end of the summer was in officers' training school. He didn't have any money, either. But she was in love with the guy, and he was in love with her, etc. She'd seen something in the paper: HELP WANTED-*Reading to Blind Man*, and a telephone number. She phoned and went over, was hired on the spot. She'd worked with this blind man all summer. She read stuff to

him, case studies, reports, that sort of thing. She helped him organize his little office in the county social-service department. They'd become good friends, my wife and the blind man. How do I know these things? She told me. And she told me something else. On her last day in the office, the blind man asked if he could touch her face. She agreed to this. She told me he touched his fingers to every part of her face, her nose ___ even her neck? She never forgot it. She even tried to write a poem about it. She was always trying to write a poem. She wrote a poem or two every year, usually after something really important had happened to her.

3　When we first started going out together, she showed me the poem. In the poem, she recalled his fingers and the way they had moved around over her face. In the poem, she talked about what she had felt at the time, about what went through her mind when the blind man touched her nose and lips. I can remember I didn't think much of the poem. Of course, I didn't tell her that. Maybe I just don't understand poetry. I admit it's not the first thing I reach for when I pick up something to read.

4　Anyway, this man who'd first enjoyed her favors, the officer-to-be, he'd been her childhood sweetheart.[1] So okay.

---

1) this man who'd first enjoyed her favors, the officer-to-be, he'd been her

I'm saying that at the end of the summer she let the blind man run his hands over her face, said good-bye to him, married her childhood etc, who was now a commissioned officer, and she moved away from Seattle.[2] But they'd kept in touch, she and the blind men. She made the first contact after a year or so. She called him up one night from an Air Force base in Alabama. She wanted to talk. They talked. He asked her to send him a tape and tell him about her life. She did this. She sent the tape. On the tape, she told the blind man about her husband and about their life together in the military. She told the blind man she loved her husband but she didn't like it where they lived and she didn't like it that he was a part of the military-industrial thing. She told the blind man she'd written a poem and he was in it. She told him that she was writing a poem about what it was like to be an Air Force officer's wife. The poem wasn't finished yet. She was still writing it. The blind man made a tape. He sent her the tape. She made a tape. This went on for years. My wife's officer was posted to one base and then another.[3] She sent tapes from

---

childhood sweetheart. 이 남자, 즉 아내의 애정을 처음으로 받게 된 남자, 예비장교는 아내의 어릴 적 sweetheart. 어릴 적 친구와 결혼을 하고 그 남자는 장교 후보생.

2) who was now a commissioned officer 그 때쯤(아내가 로버트에게 작별할 무렵)은 임관장교가 되어있었다. 공군(Air Force) 장교.

3) My wife's officer was posted to one base and then another. 아내의 남편은 한 부대에서 다른 부대로 계속 이전해 다님.

Moody AFB, McGuire, McConnell, and finally Travis, near Sacramento, where one night she got to feeling lonely and cut off from people she kept losing in that moving-around life. She got to feeling she couldn't go it another step. She went in and swallowed all the pills and capsules in the medicine chest and washed them down with a bottle of gin. Then she got into a hot bath and passed out.

5　But instead of dying, she got sick. She threw up. Her officer ___ why should he have a name? He was the childhood sweetheart, and what more does he want? — came home from somewhere, found her, and called the ambulance. In time, she put it all on a tape and sent the tape to the blind man. Over the years, she put all kinds of stuff on tapes and sent the tapes off lickety-split. Next to writing a poem every year, I think it was her chief means of recreation.[4] On one tape, she told the blind man she'd decided to live away from her officer for a time. On another tape, she told him about her divorce. She and I began going out, and of course she told her blind man about it. She told him everything, or so it seemed to me. Once she asked me if I'd like to hear the latest tape from the blind man. This was a year ago. I was on the tape, she said. So I said okay,

---

4) Next to writing a poem every year, I think it was her chief means of recreation.
매년 한 편의 시 쓰는 것 다음으로 테이프 보내기는 아내의 주된 리크리에이션 방법.

I'd listen to it. I got us drinks and we settled down in the living room. We made ready to listen. First she inserted the tape into the player and adjusted a couple of dials. Then she pushed a lever. The tape squeaked and someone began to talk in this loud voice. She lowered the volume. After a few minutes of harmless chitchat, I heard my own name in the mouth of this stranger, this blind man I didn't even know! And then this: "From all you've said about him, I can only conclude ____" But we were interrupted, a knock at the door, something, and we didn't ever get back to the tape. Maybe it was just as well.

6 Now this same blind man was coming to sleep in my house.

"Maybe I could take him bowling." I said to my wife. She was at the draining board doing scalloped potatoes.[5] She put down the knife she was using and turned around.

"If you love me." she said. "You can do this for me.[6] If you don't love me, okay. But if you had a friend, any friend, and the friend came to visit, I'd make him feel comfortable." She wiped her hands with the dish towel.

"I don't have any blind friends." I said.

"You don't have any friends." she said. "Period. Besides." she

---

5) She was at the draining board doing scalloped potatoes. 아내는 scalloped potato (감자의 종류인 듯)를 다듬으면서 개수대에 서 있었다.
6) "If you love me." she said, "you can do this for me . . ." 날 사랑하면 이 일(친구인 로버트를 맞이해서 시간을 함께 보내는 것)을 해 줄 수 있겠지.

said, "goddamn it, his wife's just died! Don't you understand that? The man's lost his wife!"

I didn't answer. She'd told me a little about the blind man's wife. Her name was Beulah. Beulah! That's a name for a colored woman.

"Was his wife a Negro?" I asked.

"Are you crazy?" My wife said. "Have you just flipped or something?"7) She picked up a potato. I saw it hit the floor, then roll under the stove. "What's wrong with you?" She said. "Are you drunk?"

"I'm just asking." I said.

Right then my wife filled me in with more detail than I cared to know.8) I made a drink and sat at the kitchen table to listen. Pieces of the story began to fall into place.9)

7 Beulah had gone to work for the blind man the summer after my wife had stopped working for him. Pretty soon Beulah and the blind man had themselves a church wedding. It was a little wedding ___ who'd want to go to such a wedding in the first place? ___ just the two of them, plus the minister and the

---

7) "Have you just flipped or something?"= Are you crazy?

8) Right then my wife filled me in with more detail than I cared to know. 내가 알고 싶은 것 이상으로 자세하게 이야기를 해 나갔다. 로버트의 결혼에 대하여 상세하게 알려줌.

9) Pieces of the story began to fall into place. 이야기 조각들이 제 자리를 찾았다. 즉 이야기를 이것저것 듣다보니 그 다음과 같은 스토리가 정리됨.

minister's wife. But it was a church wedding just the same. It was what Beulah had wanted, he'd said. But even then Beulah must have been carrying the cancer in her glands. After they had been inseparable for eight years ____ my wife's word, inseparable ____ Beulah's health went into a rapid decline. She died in a Seattle hospital room, the blind man sitting beside the bed and holding on to her hand. They'd married, lived and worked together, slept together ____ had sex, sure ____ and then the blind man had to bury her. All this without his having ever seen what the goddamned woman looked like. It was beyond my understanding. Hearing this, I felt sorry for the blind man for a little bit. And then I found myself thinking what a pitiful life this woman must have led. Imagine a woman who could never see herself as she was seen in the eyes of her loved one. A woman who could go on day after day and never received the smallest compliment from her beloved.10) A woman whose husband could never read the expression on her face, be it misery or something better.11) Someone who could wear makeup or not ____ what difference to him? She could, if she wanted, wear green eye-shadow around one eye, a straight pin in her nostril, yellow slacks, and purple shoes, no matter. And then to slip off into death, the blind man's hand on her hand, his blind eyes streaming tears ____ I'm imagining now ____ her

---

10) A woman who could go on day after day and never receive the smallest compliment from her beloved. 매일매일 살아가면서 사랑하는 사람으로부터 최소한의 칭찬도 받아 보지 못하는 여자. (남편이 blind 이므로)

11) be it misery or something better: whether it was misery or something better

last thought maybe this: that he never even knew what she looked like, and she on an express to the grave.12) Robert was left with a small insurance policy and half of a twenty-peso Mexican coin. The other half of the coin went into the box with her.13) Pathetic.

8   So when the time rolled around, my wife went to the depot to pick him up.14) With nothing to do but wait ___ sure, I blamed him for that ___ I was having a drink and watching the TV when I heard the car pull into the drive. I got up from the sofa with my drink and went to the window to have a look. I saw my wife laughing as she parked the car. I saw her get out of the car and shut the door. She was still wearing a smile. Just amazing. She went around to the other side of the car to where the blind man was already starting to get out. This blind man, feature this, he was wearing a full beard! A beard on a blind man! Too much, I say. The blind man reached into the backseat and dragged out a suitcase. My wife took his arm, shut the car door, and, talking all the way, moved him down

---

12) her last thought maybe this: that he never even knew what she looked like, and she on an express to the grave. Beulah의 마지막 생각은 (죽기 직전)은 아마도 이랬을 것이다: 남편은 내가 어떻게 생겼는지 결코 알 수 없으며 난 이제 무덤으로 직행하는군.

13) The other half of the coin went into the box with her. 멕시코 동전의 반쪽은 상자에 넣어서 Beulah의 무덤에 넣어줌.

14) When the time rolled around, my wife went to the depot to pick him up. 시간이 되었을 때 아내는 역으로 로버트를 태우러 감. 나는 남아서 기다림.

the drive and then up the steps to the front porch. I turned off the TV. I finished my drink, rinsed the glass, dried my hands. Then I went to the door.

9 My wife said, "I want you to meet Robert. Robert, this is my husband. I've told you all about him." She was beaming. She had this blind man by his coat sleeve.

The blind man let go of his suitcase and up came his hand.[15]

I took it. He squeezed hard, held my hand, and then he let it go.

"I feel like we've already met." he boomed.

"Likewise." I said I didn't know what else to say. Then I said, "Welcome. I've heard a lot about you." We began to move then, a little group, from the porch into the living room, my wife guiding him by the arm. The blind man was carrying his suitcase in his other hand. My wife said things like, "To your left here, Robert. That's right. Now watch it, there's a chair. That's it. Sit down right here. This is the sofa. We just bought this sofa two weeks ago."

I started to say something about the old sofa. I'd liked that old sofa. But I didn't say any thing. Then I wanted to say something else, small-talk, about the scenic ride along the Hudson.[16] How

---

15) The blind man let go of his suitcase and up came his hand. 옷가방을 내려놓고 손을 들었다(악수하기 위해).

going to New York, you sit on the right-hand side of the train, and coming from New York, the left-hand side.

"Did you have a good train ride?" I said. "Which side of the train did you sit on, by the way?"

"What a question, which side!" my wife said. "What's it matter which side?" she said.

"I just asked." I said.

"Right side." the blind man said. "I hadn't been on a train in nearly forty years. Not since I was a kid. With my folks. That's been a long time. I'd nearly forgotten the sensation. I have winter in my beard now.17)" he said. "So I've been told, anyway.18) Do I look distinguished, my dear?" the blind man said to my wife.

"You look distinguished, Robert." she said. "Robert." she said. "Robert, it's just so good to see you."

My wife finally took her eyes off the blind man and looked at me. I had the feeling she didn't like what she was. I shrugged.

10 I've never met, or personally known, anyone who was blind. This blind man was late forties, a heavy-set, balding man with stooped shoulders, as if he carried a great weight there.

---

16) scenic ride along the Hudson. 뉴욕의 허드슨 강을 따라가는 아름다운 기차 여행. 그래서 그 이하: 그 강을 보기 위해 뉴욕으로 갈 때는 기차의 오른 쪽에, 뉴욕에서 나올 때는 기차의 왼쪽 편에 앉아야 한다.
17) I have winter in my beard now. 이젠 수염이 허옇게 되었다.
18) So I've been told, anyway. (자신은 수염을 볼 수 없고) 다른 사람들이 그렇다 하네요.

He wore brown slacks, brown shoes, a light-brown shirt, a tie, a sports coat. Spiffy. He also had this full beard. But he didn't use a cane and he didn't wear dark glasses. I'd always thought dark glasses were a must for the blind. Fact was, I wished he had a pair.[19] At first glance, his eyes looked like anyone else's eyes. But if you looked close, there was something different about them. Too much white in the iris, for one thing, and the pupils seemed to move around in the sockets without his knowing it or being able to stop it. Creepy. As I stared at his face, I saw the left pupil turn in toward his nose while the other made an effort to keep in one place. But it was only an effort, for that eye was on the roam without his knowing it or wanting it to be.

11 I said, "Let me get you a drink. What's your pleasure? We have a little of everything. It's one of our pastimes."

"Bub, I'm a Scotch man myself." he said fast enough in this big voice.

"Right." I said. Bub! "Sure you are. I knew it."

He let his fingers touch his suitcase, which was sitting alongside the sofa. He was taking his bearings. I didn't blame him for that.

---

19) Fact was, I wished he had a pair. 로버트가 검은 안경을 쓰고 있었으면 좋겠다. a pair는 a pair of dark glasses.

"I'll move that up to your room." my wife said.

"No, that's fine." the blind man said loudly. "It can go up when I go up."

"A little water with the Scotch?" I said.

"Very little." he said.

"I knew it." I said.

He said, "Just a tad. The Irish actor, Barry Fitzgerald? I'm like that fellow. When I drink water, Fitzgerald said, I drink water. When I drink whiskey, I drink whiskey." My wife laughed. The blind man brought his hand up under his beard. He lifted his beard slowly and let it drop.

I did the drinks, three big glasses of Scotch with a splash of water in each. Then we made ourselves comfortable and talked about Robert's travels. First the long flight from the West Coast to Connecticut, we covered that.[20] Then from Connecticut up here by train.

I remembered having read somewhere that the blind didn't smoke because, as speculation had it, they couldn't see the smoke they exhaled. But this blind man smoked his cigarette down to the nubbin and then lit another one. This blind man filled his ashtray and my wife emptied it.

12 When we sat down at the table for dinner, we had

---

20) we covered that. 것은 아까 말한 바 있고.

another drink. My wife heaped Robert's plate with cube steak, scalloped potatoes, green beans. I buttered him up two slices of bread. I said, "Here's bread and butter for you." I swallowed some of my drink. "Now let us pray." I said, and the blind man lowered his head. My wife looked at me, her mouth agape. "Pray the phone won't ring and the food doesn't get cold." I said.

We dug in. We ate everything there was to eat on the table. We ate like there was no tomorrow. We didn't talk. We ate. We scarfed. We grazed that table. We were into serious eating. The blind man had right away located his foods, he knew just where everything was on his plate. I watched with admiration as he used his knife and fork on the meat. He'd cut two pieces of meat, fork the meat into his mouth, and then go all out for the scalloped potatoes, the beans next, and then he'd tear off a hunk of buttered bread and eat that. He'd follow this up with a big drink of milk. It didn't seem to bother him to use his fingers once in a while, either.

13 We finished everything, including half a strawberry pie. For a few moments, we sat as if stunned. Sweat beaded on our faces. Finally, we got up from the table and left the dirty plates. We didn't look back. We took ourselves into the living room and sank into our places again. Robert and my wife sat

on the sofa. I took the big chair. We had us two or three more drinks while they talked about the major things that had come to pass for them in the past ten years. For the most part, I just listened. Now and then I joined in. I didn't want him to think I'd left the room, and I didn't want her to think I was feeling left out. They talked of things that had happened to them ____ to them! ____ these past ten years. I waited in vain to hear my name on my wife's sweet lips: "And then my dear husband came into my life" ____ something like that. But I heard nothing of the sort. More talk of Robert. Robert had done a little of everything, it seemed, a regular blind jack-of-all trades. But most recently he and his wife had had an Amway distributorship, from which, I gathered, they'd earned their living, such as it was. The blind man was also a ham radio operator. He talked in his loud voice about conversations he'd had with fellow operators in Guam, in the Philippines, in Alaska, and even in Tahiti. He said he'd have a lot of friends there if he ever wanted to go visit those places. From time to time, he'd turn his blind face toward me, put his hand under his beard, ask me something. How long had I been in my present position? (Three years.) Did I like my work? (I didn't.) Was I going to stay with it? (What were the options?) Finally, when I thought he was beginning to run down, I got up and turned on the TV.

14　My wife looked at me with irritation. She was heading toward a boil.[21] Then she looked at the blind man and said, "Robert, do you have a TV?"

The blind man said, "My dear, I have two TVs. I have a color set and a black-and-white thing, an old relic. It's funny, but if I turn the TV on, and I'm always turning it on, I turn on the color set. It's funny, don't you think?"

I didn't know what to say to that. I had absolutely nothing to say to that. No opinion. So I watched the news program and tried to listen to what the announcer was saying.

"This is a color TV." the blind man said. "Don't ask me how, but I can tell."

"We traded up a while ago.[22]" I said.

The blind man had another taste of his drink. He lifted his beard, sniffed it, and let if fall. He leaned forward on the sofa. He positioned his ashtray on the coffee table, then put the lighter to his cigarette. He leaned back on the sofa and crossed his legs at the ankles.

My wife covered her mouth, and then she yawned. She stretched. She said, "I think I'll go upstairs and put on my robe. I think I'll change into something else. Robert, you make yourself comfortable." she said.

---

21) heading toward a boil. 폭발 직전으로 치닫고 있었다.
22) traded up. 돈을 더 주고 새것으로 바꾸었다.

"I'm comfortable." the blind man said.

"I want you to feel comfortable in this house." she said.

"I am comfortable." the blind man said.

$$\boxed{\text{II}}$$

15   After she'd left the room, he and I listened to the weather report and then to the sports roundup. By that time, she'd been gone so long I didn't know if she was going to come back. I thought she might have gone to bed. I wished she'd come back downstairs. I didn't want to be left alone with a blind man, I asked him if he wanted another drink, and he said sure. Then I asked if he wanted to smoke some dope with me, I said I'd just rolled a number. I hadn't, but I planned to do so in about two shakes.[23)]

"I'll try some with you." he said.

"Damn right." I said. "That's the stuff."

I got our drinks and sat down on the sofa with him. Then I rolled us two fat numbers. I lit one and passed it. I brought it to his fingers. He took it and inhaled.

"Hold it as long as you can." I said. I could tell he didn't know the first thing.[24)]

---

23) in about two shakes: (informal) very soon.

My wife came back downstairs wearing her pink robe and her pink slippers.

"What do I smell?" she said.

"We thought we'd have us some cannabis." I said.

My wife gave me a savage look. Then she looked at the blind man and said, "Robert, I didn't know you smoked."

He said, "I do now, my dear. There's a first time for everything. But I don't feel anything yet."

"This stuff is pretty mellow." I said. "This stuff is mild. It's dope you can reason with." I said. "It doesn't mess you up."

"Not much it doesn't, bub." he said, and laughed.

My wife sat on the sofa between the blind man and me. I passed her the number. She took it and toked and then passed it back to me. "Which way is this going?" she said. Then she said, "I shouldn't be smoking this. I can hardly keep my eyes open. That dinner did me in.25) I shouldn't have eaten so .much."

"It was the strawberry pie." the blind man said. "That's what did it." he said, and he laughed his big laugh. Then he shook his head.

"There's more strawberry pie." I said.

"Do you want some more, Robert?" my wife said.

"Maybe in a little while." he said.

---

24) I could tell he didn't know the first thing. 그가 완전 초보라는 것을 알 수 있었다.
25) do somebody in. kill or destroy.

We gave our attention to the TV. My wife yawned again. She said, "Your bed is made up when you feel like going to bed, Robert. I know you must have had a long day. When you're ready to go to bed, say so." She pulled his arm. "Robert?"

He came to[26] and said, "I've had a real nice time. This beats tapes[27], doesn't it"

I said, "Coming at you." and I put the number between his fingers. He inhaled, held the smoke, and then let it go. It was like he'd been doing it since he was nine years old.

"Thanks, bub." he said. "But I think this is all for me. I think I'm beginning to feel it." he said. He held the burning roach out for my wife.

"Same here." she said. "Ditto. Me, too." She took the roach and passed it to me. "I may just sit here for a while between you two guys with eyes closed. But don't let me bother you, okay? Either one of you. If it bothers you, say so. Otherwise, I may just sit here with my eyes closed until you're ready to go to bed." she said. "Your bed's made up, Robert, when you're ready. It's right next to our room at the top of the stairs. We'll show you up when you're ready. Wake me up, you guys, if I fall asleep." She said that and then she closed her eyes and went to sleep.

---

26) come to: recover consciousness.
27) This beats tapes. This is really exciting.

16 The news program ended. I got up and changed the channel. I sat back down on the sofa. I wished my wife hadn't pooped out. Her head lay across the back of the sofa, her mouth open. She'd turned so that her robe had slipped away from her legs, exposing a juicy thigh. I reached to draw her robe back over her, and it was then that I glanced at the blind man. What the hell! I flipped the robe open again.

"You say when you want some strawberry pie." I said.

"I will." he said.

I said, "Are you tired? Do you want me to take you up to your bed?"

"Not yet." he said. "No, I'll stay up with you, bub. If that's all right. I'll stay up until you're ready to turn in. We haven't had a chance to talk. Know what I mean? I feel like me and her monopolized the evening." He lifted his beard and he let it fall. He picked up his cigarettes and his lighter.

"That's all right." I said. Then I said, "I'm glad for the company."

17 And I guess I was. Every night I smoked dope and stayed up as long as I could before I fell asleep. My wife and I hardly ever went to bed at the same time. When I did go to sleep, I had dreams. Sometimes I'd wake up from one of them, my heart going crazy.

18 Something about the church and the Middle Ages was on the TV. I wanted to watch something else. I turned to the other channels. But there was nothing on them, either. So I turned back to the first channel and apologized.

"Bub, it's all right." the blind man said. "It's fine with me. Whatever you want to watch is okay. I'm always learning something. Learning never ends. It won't hurt me to learn something tonight. I got ears." he said.

III

19 He didn't say anything for a time. He was leaning forward with his head turned at me, his right ear aimed in the direction of the TV set.[28] Very disconcerting. Now and then his eyelids drooped and then they snapped open again. Now and then he put his fingers into his beard and tugged, like he was thinking about something he was hearing on the television.

On the screen, a group of men wearing cowls was being set upon and tormented by men dressed in skeleton costumes and men dressed as devils. The men dressed as devils wore devil masks, horns, and long tails. This pageant was part of a precession.

---

28) his right ear aimed in the direction of the set. 오른 쪽 귀를 TV set 방향으로 맞추어 놓고. 분사구문. with his right ear aimed . . .

The Englishman who was narrating the thing said it took place in Spain once a year. I tried to explain to the blind man what was happening.

"Skeletons." he said. "I know about skeletons." he said, and he nodded.

20   The TV showed this one cathedral. Then there was a long, slow look at another one. Finally, the picture switched to the famous one in Paris, with its flying buttresses and its spires reaching up to the clouds. The camera pulled away to show the whole of the cathedral rising above the skyline.

There were times when the Englishman who was telling the thing would stop, would simply let the camera move around over the cathedrals. Or else the camera would tour the countryside, men in fields walking behind oxen. I waited as long as I could.[29] Then I felt I had to say something, I said, "They're showing the outside of this cathedral now. Little statues carved to look like monsters. Now I guess they're in Italy. Yeah, they're

---

29) There was times when the Englishman who was telling the thing(대성당) would shut up, would simply let the camera move around over the cathedrals. Or else the camera would tour the countryside, men in fields walking behind oxen. 영국인 나레이터가 아무 말도 않고(shut up) 단지 카메라만이 성당 위로 빙 움직이도록 놓아두는 장면들도 있었다. 또는 카메라가 (아무 나레이션 없이) 시골을 쭉 훑어주기도 하였다. 소 뒤에서 걸어가는 들판의 사람들과 함께. 부대상황을 나타내는 분사구문이므로 with men in fields . . . 그리고 여러 차례 사용되고 있는 would는 과거의 불규칙적 습관. 이런 어색한 침묵의 시간들이 있곤 했다하는 느낌.

in Italy. There's paintings on the walls of this one church."

"Are those fresco paintings, bub?" he asked, and he sipped from his drink.

I reached for my glass. But it was empty. I tried to remember what I could remember. "You're asking me are those frescoes?" I said. "That's a good question. I don't know."

The camera moved to a cathedral outside Lisbon. The differences in the Portuguese cathedral compared with the French and Italian were not that great. But they were there. Mostly the interior stuff. Then something occurred to me, and I said, "Something has occurred to me. Do you have any idea what a cathedral is? What they look like? Do you follow me? If somebody says cathedral to you, do you have any notion what they're talking about?"

He let the smoke dribble from his mouth. "I know they took hundreds of workers fifty or a hundred years to build." he said. "I just heard the man say that, of course. I know generations of the same families worked on a cathedral. I heard him say that, too. The men who began their life's work on them, they never lived to see the completion of their work. In that sense, bub, they're no different from the rest of us, right?" He laughed. Then his eyelids drooped again. His head nodded. He seemed to be snoozing. Maybe he was imagining himself in Portugal. The TV was showing another cathedral now. This one was in

Germany. The Englishman's voice droned on. "Cathedrals." the blind man said. "If you want the truth, bub, that's about all I know. What I just said. What I heard him say. But maybe you could describe one to me? I wish you'd do it. I'd like that. If you want to know, I really don't have a good idea.

I stared hard at the shot of the cathedral on the TV. How could I even begin to describe it? But say my life depended on it. Say my life was being threatened by an insane guy who said I had to do it or else.[30]

I stared some more at the cathedral before the picture flipped off into the countryside. There was no use. I turned to the blind man and said, "To begin with, they're very tall." I was looking around the room for clues. "They reach way up. Up and up. Toward the sky. They're so big, some of them, they have to have these supports. To help hold them up, so to speak. These supports are called buttresses. They remind me of viaducts, for some reason. But you don't know viaducts, either? Sometimes the cathedrals have devils and such carved into the front. Sometimes lords and ladies. Don't ask me why this is." I said.

He was nodding. The whole upper part of his body seemed to be moving back and forth.

---

30) But say my life depended on it. Say my life was being threatened by an insane guy who said I had to do it or else. 어떤 정신 나간 자가 내 목숨을 협박하면서 꼭 해 내라고 한다면 . . . (할 수 없이 해야 하지 않겠는가?)

"I'm not doing so good, am I?" I said.

He stopped nodding and leaned forward on the edge of the sofa. As he listened to me, he was running his fingers through his beard. I wasn't getting through to him, I could see that. But he waited for me to go on just the same. He nodded, like he was trying to encourage me. I tried to think what else to say. "They're really big." I said. They're massive. They're built of stone. Marble, too, sometimes. In those olden days, when they built cathedrals, men wanted to be close to God. In those olden days, God was an important part of everyone's life. You could tell this from their cathedral building. I'm sorry." I said, "but its looks like that's the best I can do for you. I'm just no good at it."

21 "That's all right, bub." the blind man said. "Hey, listen. I hope you don't mind my asking you. Can I ask you something? Let me ask you a simple question, yes or no. I'm just curious and there's no offense. You're my host. But let me ask if you are in any way religious? You don't mind my asking?"

I shook my head. He couldn't see that, though. A wink is the same as a nod to a blind man. "I guess I don't believe in it. In anything. Sometimes it's hard. You know what I'm saying?"

"Sure, I do." he said.

"Right." I said.

The Englishman was still holding forth. My wife sighed in her sleep. She drew a long breath and went on with her sleeping.

"You'll have to forgive me." I said. "But I can't tell you what a cathedral looks like. It just isn't in me to do it. I can't do any more than I've done."

The blind man sat very still, his head down, as he listened to me.

I said, "The truth is, cathedrals don't mean anything special to me. Nothing. Cathedrals. They're something to look at on late-night TV. That's all they are."

22   It was then that the blind man cleared his throat. He took a handkerchief from his back pocket. Then he said, "I get it, bub. It's okay. It happens. Don't worry about it." he said. "Hey, listen to me. Will you do me a favor? I got an idea. Why don't you find us some heavy paper? And a pen. We'll do something. We'll draw one together. Get us a pen and some heavy paper. Go on, bub, get the stuff." he said.

So I went upstairs. My legs felt like they didn't have any strength in them. They felt like they did after I'd done some running. In my wife's room, I looked around. I found some ballpoints in a little basket on her table. And then I tried to think where to look for the kind of paper he was talking about.

Downstairs, in the kitchen, I found a shopping bag with onion skins in the bottom of the bag. I emptied the bag and shook it. I brought it into the living room and sat down with it near his legs. I moved some things, smoothed the wrinkles from the bag, spread it out on the coffee table.

The blind man got down from the sofa and sat next to me on the carpet.

He ran his fingers over the paper. He went up and down the sides of the paper. The edges, even the edges. He fingered the corners.

"All right." he said. "All right, let's do her."[31]

He found my hand, the hand with the pen. He closed his hand over my hand. "Go ahead, bub, draw." he said. "Draw. You'll see. I'll follow along with you. It'll be okay. Just begin now like I'm telling you. You'll see. Draw." The blind man said.

So I began. First I drew a box that looked like a house. It could have been the house I lived in. Then I put a roof on it. At either end of the roof, I drew spires. Crazy.

"Swell." he said. "Terrific. You're doing fine." he said. "Never thought anything like this could happen in your lifetime, did you, bub? Well, it's a strange life, we all know that. Go on now. Keep it up."

I put in windows with arches. I drew flying buttresses. I hung great doors. I couldn't stop. The TV station went off the air. I put down the pen and closed and opened my fingers. The

---

31) let's do her. 성당을 그리자. her는 성당을 가리킴.

blind man felt around over the paper, all over what I had drawn, and he nodded.

"Doing fine." the blind man said.

I took up the pen again, and he found my hand. I kept at it. I'm no artist. But I kept drawing just the same.

My wife opened up her eyes and gazed at us. She sat up on the sofa, her robe hanging open. She said, "What are you doing? Tell me, I want to know."

I didn't answer her.

The blind man said, "We're drawing a cathedral. Me and him are working on it. Press hard." he said to me. "That's right. That's good." he said. "Sure. You got it, bub. I can tell. You didn't think you could. But you can, can't you? You're cooking with gas now.[32] You know what I'm saying? We're going to really have us something here in a minute. How's the old arm?" he said. "Put some people in there now. What's a cathedral without people?"

My wife said, "What's going on? Robert, what are you doing? What's going on?"

"It's all right." he said to her. "Close your eyes now." the blind man said to me.

I did it. I closed them just like he said.

"Are they closed?" he said. "Don't fudget.[33]

---

32) You're cooking with gas now. 속어: 아주 잘하고 있다.

"They are closed." I said.

"Keep them that way." he said. He said, "Don't stop now. Draw."

So we kept on with it. His fingers rode my fingers as my hand went over the paper. It was like nothing else in my life up to now.

Then he said, "I think that's it. I think you got it." he said. "Take a look. What do you think?"

But I had my eyes closed. I thought I'd keep them that way for a little longer. I thought it was something I ought to do.

"Well?" he said. "Are you looking?"

My eyes were still closed. I was in my house. I knew that. But I didn't feel like I was inside anything.

"It's really something." I said.

---

33) Don't fudge. Don't trick.

Comprehension Check-Up Questions

1. How have the narrator's wife and the blind man kept in touch for 10 years? (section 1)

2. What prejudices does the narrator have against the blind man?

3. How did the wife and the blind man meet? (section 2)

4. What made the wife write a poem?

5. What is the narrator's opinion about the poem? Is he interested in it? (section 3)

6. What do you think caused the wife to try to commit a suicide? (section 4)

7. Considering the dialogue, do you think the narrator feels happy about the visitor? Why do you think so? (section 6)

8. Find some other prejudices the narrator has.

9. How did Robert and Beulah meet? (section 7)

10. How do you think their marriage was?

11. Why did Beulah die?

12. How does the narrator feel about Beulah? And why does he feel so?

13. The narrator still calls Robert as "the blind man." Does it mean something about his mentality or emotion toward Robert?

14. Describe the wife guiding Robert through the narrator's eyes. How does she look? Do you think this tells something about the narrator's emotions? (section 8)

15. What do you think about the conversation between Robert and the narrator? Do you think they communicate well or not? (section 9)

16. Whom do you think the wife prefers, the narrator or Robert? Why do you think so? And guess the narrator's feeling about it. What narrations reveal the narrator's emotion in this part?

17. Explain Robert's appearance. What traits of his does Robert's appearance suggest? (section 10)

18. What is the general idea of the narrator about Robert's eyes?

19. What kind of person does the dialogue show Robert to be? (section 11)

20. In what ways the wife shows her great concern about Robert again?

21. What makes the narrator amazed at Robert? (section 12)

22. Compare the communications of three characters. Who communicates well and who does not? (section 13)

23. In terms of this part, what kind of personality does Robert have? (section 14)

24. How does Robert respond when "I" offer a dope? Is it the first time for Robert to smoke it? (section 15)

25. How does the wife treat Robert in this section?

26. How do the two men feel about being left alone? (section 16)

27. How do you guess the couple's marriage life? (section 17)

28. What does Robert say when "I' apologize for watching the church on the TV? (section 18)

29. Does Robert know something about cathedral? And where did he get such knowledge?

30. How does the narrator feel about explaining the cathedral to Robert? And how does Robert respond to his explanation? (section 20)

31. Is the narrator a religious man? (section 21)

The Monkey's Paw

W.W. Jacobs

William Wymark Jacobs (1863–1943), an English author of short stories and novels. Although much of his work was humorous, he is most famous for his horror story "The Monkey's Paw." Jacobs was born in Wapping, London; his father was wharf manager at the South Devon wharf at Lower East Smithfield. He was educated at a private school in London and later at Birkbeck College. In 1879, Jacobs began work as a clerk in the civil service, and by 1885 he had had his first short story published. Jacobs is now remembered for his macabre tale "The Monkey's Paw" (published 1902 in the collection of short stories *The Lady of the Barge*) and "The Toll House" (published 1909 in the collection of short stories *Sailors' Knots*). However, the majority of his output was humorous in tone. Jacobs married soon after his success. His wife, a militant suffragette and socialist, was very different from the conservative Jacobs, and their marriage was not a happy one. This fact may have contributed to the negative depiction of women that runs through most of his fiction. Jacobs died at Hornsey Lane, Islington, London, in 1943.

"The Monkey's Paw" is a supernatural short story by author W. W. Jacobs first published in England in the collection *The Lady of the Barge* in 1902. In the story, three wishes are granted to the owner of the monkey's paw, but the wishes come with an enormous price for interfering with fate. It has been adapted scores of times in other media, including plays, films, TV series, operas, stories and comics, as early as 1903 and as recently as 2017.

The short story involves Mr. and Mrs. White and their adult son, Herbert. Sergeant-Major Morris, a friend who served with the British Army in India, introduces them to a mummified monkey's paw. An old fakir placed a spell on the paw, so that it would grant three wishes. The wishes are granted but always with hellish consequences as punishment for tampering with fate. Morris, having had a horrific experience using the paw, throws the monkey's paw into the fire but Mr. White retrieves it. Before leaving, Morris warns Mr. White that if he does use the paw, then it will be on his own head. The story subsequently shows how Mr.White's admonition horribly turns into life (*adapted from Wikipedia*).

Vocabulary	
parlour	henpecked
placidly	maligned
hark at	mar
amiably	simian

bawl	prosaic
bog	frivolous
burly	avaricious
rubicund of visage	scurry
sergeant-Major	bibulous
tum	furtively
doughty	interpose
a slip of a youth	steep in
fakir	apathy
leastways	subdue
off-handedly	quaking
fumbling	aghast
proffer	mutilate
jarred	pulsating
presumptuous	hoarsely
blotchy	wrench
doggedly	stiffly
talisman	fusillade
gruffly	reverberate
enthrall	frantically
shan't - shall not	wail

I

Outside, the night was cold and wet, but in the small parlour of Laburnam Villa the blinds were drawn and the fire burned brightly. Father and son were at chess, the former, who possessed ideas about the game involving radical changes, putting his king into such sharp and unnecessary perils that it even provoked comment from the white-haired old lady knitting placidly by the fire.

"Hark[1] at the wind." said Mr. White, who, having seen a fatal mistake after it was too late, was amiably desirous of preventing his son from seeing it.

"I'm listening." said the latter, grimly surveying the board as he stretched out his hand. "Check."[2]

"I should hardly think that he'd come tonight." said his father, with his hand poised over the board.

"Mate."[3] replied the son.

"That's the worst of living so far out." bawled Mr. White, with sudden and unlooked-for violence;"[4] of all the beastly, slushy, out-of-the-way places to live in, this is the worst. Pathway's a bog, and the road's a torrent. I don't know what people are

---

1) listen의 고어.
2) "Check." 체스 둘 때 쓰는 용어.
3) "Mate." 또 다른 체스 용어.
4) with sudden and unlooked-for violence 갑자기 폭력적으로.

thinking about. I suppose because only two houses on the road are let, they think it doesn't matter."

"Never mind, dear." said his wife soothingly; "perhaps you'll win the next one."

Mr. White looked up sharply, just in time to intercept a knowing glance between mother and son.[5] The words died away on his lips, and he hid a guilty grin in his thin grey beard.

"There he is." said Herbert White, as the gate banged to loudly and heavy footsteps came toward the door.

The old man rose with hospitable haste, and opening the door, was heard condoling with the new arrival. The new arrival also condoled with himself, so that Mrs. White said, "Tut, tut!" and coughed gently as her husband entered the room, followed by a tall burly man, beady of eye and rubicund of visage.

"Sergeant-Major Morris." he said, introducing him.

The sergeant-major shook hands, and taking the proffered seat by the fire, watched contentedly while his host got out whisky and tumblers and stood a small copper kettle on the fire.

At the third glass his eyes got brighter, and he began to talk, the little family circle regarding with eager interest this visitor from distant parts, as he squared his broad shoulders in the chair and spoke of strange scenes and doughty deeds; of wars

---

5) just in time to intercept a knowing glance between mother and son 모자간에 서로 통하는 시선을 제때 알아차리고서. intercept는 갑작스레 낚아채는 동작.

and plagues and strange peoples.

"Twenty-one years of it." said Mr. White, nodding at his wife and son. "When he went away he was a slip of a youth in the warehouse. Now look at him."

"He don't look to have taken much harm." said Mrs. White, politely.

"I'd like to go to India myself." said the old man, "just to look round a bit, you know."

"Better where you are." said the sergeant-major, shaking his head. He put down the empty glass, and sighing softly, shook it again.

"I should like to see those old temples and fakirs and jugglers." said the old man. "What was that you started telling me the other day about a monkey's paw or something, Morris?"

"Nothing." said the soldier hastily. "Leastways, nothing worth hearing."

"Monkey's paw?" said Mrs. White curiously.

"Well, it's just a bit of what you might call magic, perhaps." said the sergeant-major off-handedly.

His three listeners leaned forward eagerly. The visitor absentmindedly put his empty glass to his lips and then set it down again. His host filled it for him.

"To look at." said the sergeant-major, fumbling in his pocket, "it's just an ordinary little paw, dried to a mummy."

He took something out of his pocket and proffered it. Mrs. White drew back with a grimace, but her son, taking it, examined it curiously.

"And what is there special about it?" inquired Mr. White, as he took it from his son and, having examined it, placed it upon the table.

"It had a spell put on it by an old fakir." said the sergeant-major, "a very holy man. He wanted to show that fate ruled people's lives, and that those who interfered with it did so to their sorrow. He put a spell on it so that three separate men could each have three wishes from it."

His manner was so impressive that his hearers were conscious that their light laughter jarred somewhat.

"Well, why don't you have three, sir?" said Herbert White cleverly.

The soldier regarded him in the way that middle age is wont to regard presumptuous youth. "I have." he said quietly, and his blotchy face whitened.

"And did you really have the three wishes granted?" asked Mrs. White.

"I did." said the sergeant-major, and his glass tapped against his strong teeth.

"And has anybody else wished?" inquired the old lady.

"The first man had his three wishes, yes." was the reply.

"I don't know what the first two were, but the third was for death. That's how I got the paw."

His tones were so grave that a hush fell upon the group.

"If you've had your three wishes, it's no good to you now, then, Morris." said the old man at last. "What do you keep it for?"

The soldier shook his head. "Fancy, I suppose." he said slowly.

"If you could have another three wishes." said the old man, eyeing him keenly, "would you have them?"

"I don't know." said the other. "I don't know."

He took the paw, and dangling it between his front finger and thumb, suddenly threw it upon the fire. White, with a slight cry, stooped down and snatched it off.

"Better let it burn." said the soldier solemnly.

"If you don't want it, Morris." said the old man, "give it to me."

"I won't." said his friend doggedly. "I threw it on the fire. If you keep it, don't blame me for what happens. Pitch it on the fire again, like a sensible man."

The other shook his head and examined his new possession closely. "How do you do it?" he inquired.

"Hold it up in your right hand and wish aloud,' said the sergeant-major, "but I warn you of the consequences."

"Sounds like the Arabian Nights." said Mrs White, as she rose and began to set the supper. "Don't you think you might wish for four pairs of hands for me?"

Her husband drew the talisman from his pocket and then all three burst into laughter as the sergeant-major, with a look of alarm on his face, caught him by the arm.

"If you must wish." he said gruffly, "wish for something sensible."

Mr. White dropped it back into his pocket, and placing chairs, motioned his friend to the table. In the business of supper the talisman was partly forgotten, and afterward the three sat listening in an enthralled fashion to a second instalment of the soldier's adventures in India.

"If the tale about the monkey paw is not more truthful than those he has been telling us." said Herbert, as the door closed behind their guest, just in time for him to catch the last train, "we shan't make much out of it."

"Did you give him anything for it, father?" inquired Mrs. White, regarding her husband closely.

"A trifle." said he, colouring slightly. "He didn't want it, but I made him take it. And he pressed me again to throw it away."

"Likely." said Herbert, with pretended horror. "Why, we're going to be rich, and famous, and happy. Wish to be an emperor, father, to begin with; then you can't be henpecked."

He darted round the table, pursued by the maligned Mrs. White armed with an antimacassar.

Mr. White took the paw from his pocket and eyed it dubiously.

"I don't know what to wish for, and that's a fact." he said slowly. "It seems to me I've got all I want."

"If you only cleared the house,[6] you'd be quite happy, wouldn't you?" said Herbert, with his hand on his shoulder. "Well, wish for two hundred pounds, then; that'll just do it."

His father, smiling shamefacedly at his own credulity, held up the talisman, as his son, with a solemn face somewhat marred by a wink at his mother, sat down at the piano and struck a few impressive chords.[7]

"I wish for two hundred pounds." said the old man distinctly.

A fine crash from the piano greeted the words, interrupted by a shuddering cry from the old man. His wife and son ran toward him.

"It moved, he cried, with a glance of disgust at the object as it lay on the floor. "As I wished it twisted in my hands like a snake."

"Well, I don't see the money." said his son, as he picked it up and placed it on the table, "and I bet I never shall."

"It must have been your fancy, father." said his wife, regarding him anxiously.

He shook his head. "Never mind, though; there's no harm

---

6) clear the house 집 대출금을 청산하다.

7) His father, smiling shamefacedly at his own credulity 자신이 그 talisman을 믿는다는 사실에 대해 부끄러워 미소 지으면서, held up the talisman, //as his son, with a solemn face somewhat marred by a wink at his mother, 아들은 심각한 얼굴을 하고서(그런데 그 얼굴은 어머니에게 윙크하느라 다소 형태가 찌그러짐)피아노 앞에 앉았을 때.

done, but it gave me a shock all the same."

They sat down by the fire again while the two men finished their pipes. Outside, the wind was higher than ever, and the old man started nervously at the sound of a door banging upstairs. A silence unusual and depressing settled upon all three, which lasted until the old couple rose to retire for the night.

"I expect you'll find the cash tied up in a big bag in the middle of your bed." said Herbert, as he bade them good-night, "and something horrible squatting up on top of the wardrobe watching you as you pocket your ill-gotten gains."[8]

He sat alone in the darkness, gazing at the dying fire, and seeing faces in it. The last face was so horrible and so simian that he gazed at it in amazement. It got so vivid that, with a little uneasy laugh, he felt on the table for a glass containing a little water to throw over it.[9] His hand grasped the monkey's paw, and with a little shiver he wiped his hand on his coat and went up to bed.

---

8) something horrible squatting up on top of the wardrobe watching you as you pocket your ill-gotten gains 아버지(you)가 불로소득(즉 2000 파운드)을 호주머니에 넣을 때 옷장 꼭대기에 웅크리고 앉은 끔찍한 것(즉 monkey's paw)이 아버지를 빤히 쳐다보고 있을 거예요.

9) It 벽난로 불빛 속으로 보이는 괴기한 웃는 얼굴 got so vivid that, with a little uneasy laugh 불편한 웃음을 웃으며, he felt on the table for a glass containing a little water to throw over it 웃는 얼굴 위로 물을 끼얹기 위해 물이 약간 든 컵을 찾아 테이블 위를 더듬더듬하다. 이 이야기에서 "feel"을 더듬더듬 찾다라는 의미로 자주 사용됨. His hand grasped the monkey's paw,(물컵 대신) monkey's paw가 손에 잡혀서 and with a little shiver he wiped his hand on his coat 몸을 부르르 떨며 그 손을 옷에 닦았다 and went up to bed.

II

In the brightness of the wintry sun next morning as it streamed over the breakfast table Herbert laughed at his fears. There was an air of prosaic wholesomeness about the room which it had lacked on the previous night, and the dirty, shrivelled little paw was pitched on the sideboard with a carelessness which betokened no great belief in its virtues.10)

"I suppose all old soldiers are the same." said Mrs White. "The idea of our listening to such nonsense! How could wishes be granted in these days? And if they could, how could two hundred pounds hurt you, father?"

"Might drop on his head from the sky." said the frivolous Herbert.

"Morris said the things happened so naturally." said his father, "that you might if you so wished attribute it to coincidence."

"Well, don't break into the money before I come back." said Herbert, as he rose from the table. "I'm afraid it'll turn you into a mean, avaricious man, and we shall have to disown you."

His mother laughed, and following him to the door, watched

---

10) the dirty, shrivelled little paw was pitched on the sideboard with a carelessness which betokened no great belief in its virtues. 더럽고 쪼그라든 작은 paw가 찬장 위에 아무렇게나(without carelessness) 얹혀 있었다. 그 virtue(여기서는 영험한 효력)를 전혀 믿지 않는 것을 의미하는 듯한 아무렇게나 놓인 모양. 즉 하도 아무렇게나 던져 놓아서 누구도 그것이 신기한 영물임을 믿지 않는 듯이 취급해 놓았다는 뜻.

him down the road, and returning to the breakfast table, was very happy at the expense of her husband's credulity. All of which did not prevent her from scurrying to the door at the postman's knock, nor prevent her from referring somewhat shortly to retired sergeant-majors of bibulous habits when she found that the post brought a tailor's bill.[11]

"Herbert will have some more of his funny remarks, I expect, when he comes home." she said, as they sat at dinner.

"I dare say." said Mr. White, pouring himself out some beer; "but for all that, the thing moved in my hand; that I'll swear to."

"You thought it did." said the old lady soothingly.

"I say it did." replied the other. "There was no thought about it; I had just — What's the matter?"

His wife made no reply. She was watching the mysterious movements of a man outside, who, peering in an undecided fashion at the house, appeared to be trying to make up his mind to enter. In mental connection with the two hundred pounds, she noticed that the stranger was well dressed and

---

11) was very happy at the expense of her husband's credulity 남편의 credulity(monkey's paw의 효능을 은근히 믿음)를 막 놀리면서 즐거워했다. All of which 앞의 사실/즉 남편이 쉽게 남의 말을 믿는다는 것을 놀림 did not prevent her from scurrying to the door at the postman's knock, nor prevent her from referring somewhat shortly to retired sergeant-majors of bibulous habits when she found that the post brought a tailor's bill. 남편의 credulity를 놀리면서도 아내 자신도 역시 우편부의 노크소리에 얼른 문으로 뛰어가거나, 음주습관이 있는 은퇴한 sergent-major들 이야기를 잠깐잠깐 했다(Morris가 생각나서). 그 때 온 우편배달부는 (두 사람이 은근히 기대하던 돈 2000 파운드가 아니라 단순한) 청구서를 가져옴.

wore a silk hat of glossy newness. Three times he paused at the gate, and then walked on again. The fourth time he stood with his hand upon it, and then with sudden resolution flung it open and walked up the path. Mrs. White at the same moment placed her hands behind her, and hurriedly unfastening the strings of her apron, put that useful article of apparel beneath the cushion of her chair.12)

She brought the stranger, who seemed ill at ease, into the room. He gazed at her furtively, and listened in a preoccupied fashion as the old lady apologized for the appearance of the room, and her husband's coat, a garment which he usually reserved for the garden. She then waited as patiently as her sex would permit, for him to broach his business, but he was at first strangely silent.

"I — was asked to call." he said at last, and stooped and picked a piece of cotton from his trousers. "I come from Maw and Meggins."

The old lady started. "Is anything the matter?" she asked

---

12) The fourth time he stood with his hand upon it, and then with sudden resolution flung it open and walked up the path. Mrs. White at the same moment placed her hands behind her, and hurriedly unfastening the strings of her apron, put that useful article of apparel beneath the cushion of her chair(문을 열까 말까 망설이다 세 번이나 돌아서던 회사직원이) 네 번 째로 오더니 문 위에 손을 얹고 섰다. 그리고는 갑작스런 결심을 하고는 문을 열고 복도로 들어왔다. 그 순간 미스즈 화이트는 손을 등 뒤로 해서 부랴부랴 앞치마 끈을 풀고는 그 유용한 천(늘 사용하는 앞치마)을 쿠션 뒤에 내려놓았다.

breathlessly. "Has anything happened to Herbert? What is it? What is it?"

Her husband interposed. "There, there, mother." he said hastily. "Sit down, and don't jump to conclusions. You've not brought bad news, I'm sure, sir" and he eyed the other wistfully.

"I'm sorry — " began the visitor.

"Is he hurt?" demanded the mother.

The visitor bowed in assent. "Badly hurt." he said quietly, "but he is not in any pain."

"Oh, thank God!" said the old woman, clasping her hands. "Thank God for that! Thank — "

She broke off suddenly as the sinister meaning of the assurance dawned upon her and she saw the awful confirmation of her fears in the other's averted face.13) She caught her breath, and turning to her slower-witted husband, laid her trembling old hand upon his. There was a long silence.

"He was caught in the machinery." said the visitor at length, in a low voice.

"Caught in the machinery." repeated Mr. White, in a dazed

---

13) She broke off suddenly as the sinister meaning of the assurance dawned upon her and she saw the awful confirmation of her fears in the other's averted face. 그 끔찍한 확인의 의미(허버트가 더 이상 고통을 느끼지 않는다는 확인/즉 사망)가 무엇인지 미시즈 화이트에게 떠오르자 그녀는 갑자기 말을 끊고 (회사 직원을 바라보는데) 그 직원의 살짝 돌리는 (averted/피하다) 얼굴에서 자신이 두려워하는 것(혹시 허버트가?)에 대한 확인을 읽고는 . . .

fashion, "yes."

He sat staring blankly out at the window, and taking his wife's hand between his own, pressed it as he had been wont to do in their old courting days nearly forty years before.

"He was the only one left to us." he said, turning gently to the visitor. "It is hard."

The other coughed, and rising, walked slowly to the window. "The firm wished me to convey their sincere sympathy with you in your great loss." he said, without looking round. "I beg that you will understand I am only their servant and merely obeying orders."

There was no reply; the old woman's face was white, her eyes staring, and her breath inaudible; on the husband's face was a look such as his friend the sergeant might have carried into his first action.

"I was to say that Maw and Meggins disclaim all responsibility, "14) continued the other. "They admit no liability at all, but in consideration of your son's services they wish to present you with a certain sum as compensation."

Mr. White dropped his wife's hand, and rising to his feet, gazed with a look of horror at his visitor. His dry lips shaped the words, "How much?"

---

14) I was to say that Maw and Meggins disclaim all responsibility. Maw and Meggins 회사는 책임이 없다는 점을 말씀드려야겠습니다. be to 용법: 여기서는 should.

"Two hundred pounds." was the answer.

Unconscious of his wife's shriek, the old man smiled faintly, put out his hands like a sightless man, and dropped, a senseless heap, to the floor.[15]

III

In the huge new cemetery, some two miles distant, the old people buried their dead, and came back to a house steeped in shadow and silence. It was all over so quickly that at first they could hardly realize it, and remained in a state of expectation as though of something else to happen — something else which was to lighten this load, too heavy for old hearts to bear.[16]

But the days passed, and expectation gave place to resignation[17]

---

15) Unconscious of his wife's shriek, the old man smiled faintly, put out his hands like a sightless man, and dropped, a senseless heap, to the floor. 아내의 목소리는 들리지 않고, 화이트씨는 희미하게 웃으며 두 손을 마치 앞이 보이지 않는 사람처럼 허우적거리며 마루에 털썩 무너져 내렸다. 그 때 모습이 senseless heap처럼 보임. 여기서 being a senseless heap: 분사구문. senseless heap이 되면서 무너졌다는 느낌.

16) It was all over so quickly that at first they could hardly realize it, and remained in a state of expectation as though of something else to happen — something else which was to lighten this load, too heavy for old hearts to bear. 사건이 너무 빨리 끝나버려서 부부는 그 사건이 무엇인지 알아차리기도 힘들었다. 그 다음에는 다른 일이 일어나기라도 할 것 같은 기대 상태에 빠져 있었다. 다른 사건이란 그 짐(사고 후의 엄청난 마음의 무거움), 두 나이든 사람이 감내하기에 너무 무거운 짐, 그 짐을 가볍게 해 줄 수 있는 어떤 일이 일어날 것을 기대. be to 용법.

— the hopeless resignation of the old, sometimes miscalled, apathy. Sometimes they hardly exchanged a word, for now they had nothing to talk about, and their days were long to weariness.

It was about a week after that that the old man, waking suddenly in the night, stretched out his hand and found himself alone. The room was in darkness, and the sound of subdued weeping came from the window. He raised himself in bed and listened.

"Come back." he said tenderly. "You will be cold."

"It is colder for my son." said the old woman, and wept afresh.

The sound of her sobs died away on his ears. The bed was warm, and his eyes heavy with sleep. He dozed fitfully, and then slept until a sudden wild cry from his wife awoke him with a start.

"The paw!" she cried wildly. "The monkey's paw!"

He started up in alarm. "Where? Where is it? What's the matter?"

She came stumbling across the room toward him. "I want it." she said quietly. "You've not destroyed it?"

"It's in the parlour, on the bracket." he replied, marvelling. "Why?"

She cried and laughed together, and bending over, kissed his

---

17) But the days passed, and expectation gave place to resignation. 하지만 시간이 흐르면서 기대가 체념으로 바뀜.

cheek.

"I only just thought of it." she said hysterically. "Why didn't I think of it before? Why didn't you think of it?"

"Think of what?" he questioned.

"The other two wishes." she replied rapidly. "We've only had one."

"Was not that enough?" he demanded fiercely.

"No." she cried, triumphantly; "we'll have one more. Go down and get it quickly, and wish our boy alive again."

The man sat up in bed and flung the bedclothes from his quaking limbs. "Good God, you are mad!" he cried aghast.

"Get it." she panted; "get it quickly, and wish — Oh, my boy, my boy!"

Her husband struck a match and lit the candle. "Get back to bed." he said, unsteadily. "You don't know what you are saying."

"We had the first wish granted." said the old woman, feverishly; "why not the second."

"A coincidence." stammered the old man.

"Go and get it and wish." cried the old woman, quivering with excitement.

The old man turned and regarded her, and his voice shook. "He has been dead ten days, and besides he — I would not tell you else, but — I could only recognize him by his clothing. If he was too terrible for you to see then, how now?"

"Bring him back." cried the old woman, and dragged him toward the door. "Do you think I fear the child I have nursed?"

He went down in the darkness, and felt his way to the parlour, and then to the mantelpiece. The talisman was in its place, and a horrible fear that the unspoken wish might bring his mutilated son before him ere he could escape from the room seized upon him, and he caught his breath as he found that he had lost the direction of the door. His brow cold with sweat, he felt his way round the table, and groped along the wall until he found himself in the small passage with the unwholesome thing in his hand.[18]

Even his wife's face seemed changed as he entered the room. It was white and expectant, and to his fears seemed to have an unnatural look upon it. He was afraid of her.

"Wish!" she cried, in a strong voice.

"It is foolish and wicked." he faltered.

---

18) a horrible fear that the unspoken wish might bring his mutilated son before him ere he could escape from the room seized upon him, and he caught his breath as he found that he had lost the direction of the door. His brow cold with sweat, he felt his way round the table, and groped along the wall until he found himself in the small passage with the unwholesome thing in his hand. 아직 말해지지 않는 소원 — 지금 아내의 강권으로 아래층에 내려와 monkey's paw를 가지러 옴. 두 번째 소원을 말하기 위해. 그래서 여기서 the unspoken wish는 앞으로 이야기하게 될 것 같은 두 번째 소원 — 이 그의 죽은 아들을 눈앞에 데리고 올 것이라는 끔찍한 공포 — 미처 도망가기도 전에 시체가 살아서 나타날 것이라는 — 가 화이트 씨를 엄습. 테이블을 더듬더듬해서 벽을 더듬다가 드디어 그 불길한 것(monkey's paw)을 손에 들고 작은 복도에 서 있게 된 자신을 발견.

"Wish!" repeated his wife.

He raised his hand. "I wish my son alive again."

The talisman fell to the floor, and he regarded it fearfully. Then he sank trembling into a chair as the old woman, with burning eyes, walked to the window and raised the blind.

He sat until he was chilled with the cold, glancing occasionally at the figure of the old woman peering through the window. The candle end, which had burnt below the rim of the china candlestick, was throwing pulsating shadows on the ceiling and walls, until, with a flicker larger than the rest, it expired. The old man, with an unspeakable sense of relief at the failure of the talisman, crept back to his bed, and a minute or two afterward the old woman came silently and apathetically beside him.

Neither spoke, but both lay silently listening to the ticking of the clock. A stair creaked, and a squeaky mouse scurried noisily through the wall. The darkness was oppressive, and after lying for some time screwing up his courage, the husband took the box of matches, and striking one, went downstairs for a candle.[19]

At the foot of the stairs the match went out, and he paused to strike another, and at the same moment a knock, so quiet and

---

19) after lying for some time screwing up his courage, the husband took the box of matches, and striking one, went downstairs for a candle: 얼마간(for some time) 용기를 쥐어짜내느라 누워 있다가, 마침내 성냥통을 들고 성냥 하나를 켠 뒤, 아래층으로 초를 찾아 내려감.

stealthy as to be scarcely audible, sounded on the front door.

The matches fell from his hand. He stood motionless, his breath suspended until the knock was repeated. Then he turned and fled swiftly back to his room, and closed the door behind him. A third knock sounded through the house.

"What's that?" cried the old woman, starting up.

"A rat." said the old man, in shaking tones — "a rat. It passed me on the stairs."

His wife sat up in bed listening. A loud knock resounded through the house.

"It's Herbert!" she screamed. "It's Herbert!"

She ran to the door, but her husband was before her, and catching her by the arm, held her tightly.

"What are you going to do?" he whispered hoarsely.

"It's my boy; it's Herbert!" she cried, struggling mechanically. "I forgot it was two miles away. What are you holding me for? Let go. I must open the door."

"For God's sake, don't let it in." cried the old man trembling.

"You're afraid of your own son." she cried, struggling. "Let me go. I'm coming, Herbert; I'm coming."

There was another knock, and another. The old woman with a sudden wrench broke free and ran from the room. Her husband followed to the landing, and called after her appealingly as she hurried downstairs. He heard the chain rattle back and the bottom bolt drawn slowly and stiffly from the socket.[20] Then the old woman's voice, strained and panting.

"The bolt." she cried loudly. "Come down. I can't reach it."

But her husband was on his hands and knees groping wildly on the floor in search of the paw. If he could only find it before the thing outside got in. A perfect fusillade of knocks reverberated through the house, and he heard the scraping of a chair as his wife put it down in the passage against the door. He heard the creaking of the bolt as it came slowly back, and at the same moment he found the monkey's paw, and frantically breathed his third and last wish.

The knocking ceased suddenly, although the echoes of it were still in the house. He heard the chair drawn back and the door opened. A cold wind rushed up the staircase, and a long loud wail of disappointment and misery from his wife gave him courage to run down to her side, and then to the gate beyond. The street lamp flickering opposite shone on a quiet and deserted road.

---

20) The old woman with a sudden wrench broke free 갑자기 몸을 비틀어(wrench: 지금 미스터 화이트가 붙잡고 있는 상태) 자유롭게 벗어나서는 and ran from the room. Her husband followed to the landing, and called after her appealingly 아내를 애절히 부르며 따라갔다 as she hurried downstairs. He heard the chain rattle back and the bottom bolt drawn slowly and stiffly from the socket. 문을 걸어 잠근 사슬이 스르르 소리를 내며 풀리면서 아래쪽 걸쇠(bolt)가 천천히 뻑뻑한 소리를 내며 소켓(걸쇠를 걸어 둔 장치)에서 빠져나오는 소리가 들렸다. bolt가 뻑뻑해서 잘 안 빠져나오는 상태.

Comprehension Check-Up Questions

1. What spell was put on the monkey's paw by a fakir?
   Why did the fakir put the spell on the paw? (Part I)

2. What is Mr.White's first wish?

3. Why does Mr White make a second wish? What is it? (Part II)

4. Why does Mr.White make a third wish? (Part III)

5. Did they see Herbert come back alive from the grave?
   Why or why not? And what is the horrible effect of the very last scene?